W9-CPH-552

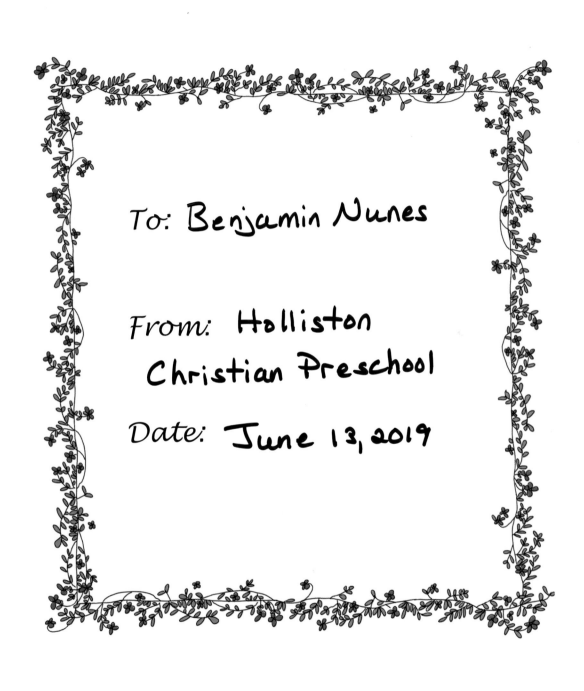

To: Benjamin Nunes

From: Holliston Christian Preschool

Date: June 13, 2019

For God so loved the world, that he gave his only son,
that whoever believes in him should not perish,
but have eternal life.

John 3:16

The Jesus Bible for kids

The Jesus Bible for Kids
© 2015 (North America) International Publishing Services
Pty Ltd Sydney Australia
www.ipsoz.com
External Markets © North Parade Publishing
Written by Janice Emmerson
Illustrations by QBS Learning

Published by Harvest House Publishers
Eugene, Oregon 97402
www.harvesthousepublishers.com

ISBN 978-0-7369-6721-1

Printed in China

15 16 17 18 19 20 21 22 23 / IPS / 11 10 9 8 7 6 5 4 3 2 1

The Jesus Bible for kids

stories from the New Testament
retold by Janice Emmerson

HARVEST HOUSE PUBLISHERS
EUGENE, OREGON

Contents

A Visit by an Angel

Mary lived in the village of Nazareth, halfway between the Sea of Galilee and the Mediterranean Sea. Not much went on in Nazareth, for it was small and unimportant, but Mary was happy and excited, for she was engaged to be married to Joseph, a carpenter who could trace his family back to King David.

Now, one day, Mary was quietly going about her chores when suddenly she was aware of a bright light shining before her, and she looked up to see an angel of God, all in white. She gasped in shock— what could this mean? But the angel smiled at her and said gently, "Mary, don't be afraid. God loves you and has blessed you. He has chosen you for a very special honor. You will give birth to a baby boy, and you are to call him Jesus. He will be called the Son of God, and his kingdom will never end!"

Mary was filled with wonder. "How can this be?" she asked softly. "I'm not even married!"

"Nothing is impossible for God," replied the angel. "The Holy Spirit will come on you, and your child will be God's own Son."

Mary could hardly believe what she was hearing, but she trusted God with all her heart. If he said it would happen, it would happen.

"I am God's servant," she said. "I'll do whatever God wants me to."

God spoke to Joseph in a dream and explained that Mary had not been unfaithful to him and that the child would be very special indeed. Joseph married Mary straight away and took good care of her.

An Important Journey

Soon it would be time for Mary to have her baby. She probably wanted to be nice and comfortable in her own home, with all her own things around her and her family nearby to help out. But that wasn't how it worked out.

You see, at exactly this time, the emperor of Rome decided to order a census. The emperor was a very powerful man, and he ruled over many, many lands. He wanted to keep track of every single person in all the lands that he ruled over. He wanted to make sure that everyone paid their taxes! And so all the people throughout the lands ruled by Rome had to go to their hometown to be counted.

It so happened that Joseph's family was descended from King David, and so he and Mary had to travel to Bethlehem, where King David had been born. Mary's baby was due to be born any day, and the journey was long and hard, but like everyone else, they had to do as the emperor ordered.

When Mary and Joseph finally arrived in Bethlehem, they were tired and desperately wanted to find a room for the night, for the time had come for Mary's baby to be born.

But the town was filled to bursting, for everyone had come to be counted. The houses were crowded as families squeezed in, and as for the inns, well, every single room in every single inn was full. By the time that Joseph and Mary arrived in Bethlehem, there was nowhere for them to stay!

Things seemed very bleak, but at last, one kind innkeeper took pity on them.

"I'm afraid I have no rooms free, but if you don't mind a bit of straw, I do have somewhere that you can spend the night," he said, and he showed them to a stable where the animals were kept. It was dirty and smelly, but it was the best they could do.

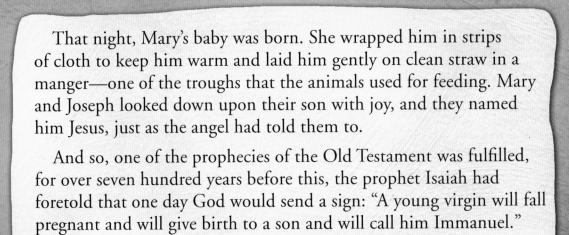

That night, Mary's baby was born. She wrapped him in strips of cloth to keep him warm and laid him gently on clean straw in a manger—one of the troughs that the animals used for feeding. Mary and Joseph looked down upon their son with joy, and they named him Jesus, just as the angel had told them to.

And so, one of the prophecies of the Old Testament was fulfilled, for over seven hundred years before this, the prophet Isaiah had foretold that one day God would send a sign: "A young virgin will fall pregnant and will give birth to a son and will call him Immanuel."

You see, Immanuel means "God is with us," and that is exactly what had happened—God had come to live with us on earth. Jesus was Immanuel!

The Very First Visitors

That same night, on a hillside overlooking Bethlehem, some shepherds were watching over their sheep. Apart from keeping an eye out for wild animals, there wasn't much to do, so they sat around a fire sharing stories.

All of a sudden, the dark night sky was ablaze with light, and the shepherds fell to the ground in fright as an angel of the Lord appeared in the sky above them.

"Don't be afraid," the angel said to them gently, just as he had reassured Mary so many months ago. "I am here to bring you good news—the best news! Today a very special baby has been born in King David's town—he is Christ, the Messiah, God's own Son! Go and see for yourselves. You will find him lying in a manger in a stable."

And with these words the sky was filled with more angels, all singing a wonderful, beautiful song praising God: "Glory to God in the highest heaven, and peace on earth and good will to all men!"

And then, as swiftly as they had come, the angels disappeared.

19

In the silence that followed, the shepherds looked at one another in amazement. Had that really just happened? Had a host of shining angels just appeared to them, a bunch of dirty, raggedy shepherds?

But they didn't waste much time thinking about "why?" for they were far too busy racing down to the town and searching for the stable where they would find the special baby. And when they did find Mary and Joseph, and little Jesus lying in the manger just as they had been told, their hearts exploded with joy and gratitude, and they rushed off to tell everyone they could find about the wonderful news.

21

Following a Star

In a distant land far to the east, three wise men had been studying the stars. These men were clever and respected and wealthy—you might even have mistaken them for kings if you had seen them in all their finery!

Anyway, one night they discovered a bright new star shining in the skies. They knew that it meant something very special—they knew that it was a sign that a great king had been born—and so they prepared for a long journey, packed up their things, and followed the star all the way to Jerusalem.

In Jerusalem they made their way to the court of Herod the Great (who wasn't really so great, for he was actually rather cruel and wicked), who was the king of Judea (although really he had to do what the Roman emperor told him to do). There they asked if he could show them the way to the baby who would be the king of the Jews.

Herod was horrified! He was king—he didn't want another king around! His advisors told him of a prophecy that the new king would be born in the city of King David, in Bethlehem.

Then the cunning king sent the wise men to Bethlehem, saying, "Once you have found him, come back and tell me where he is so that I can visit him too!" He didn't say what sort of visit he wanted to pay him!

The wise men followed the star all the way to a humble house. There they found Jesus and his parents. Though he was only a little child, these wise and powerful men knelt down before him and presented him with fine gifts of gold, sweet-smelling frankincense, and a spicy ointment called myrrh before returning home. But they did not stop off at Herod's palace, for God had warned them in a dream not to go there.

When King Herod realized that they weren't coming back, he was furious. He was so angry that he gave an order that every boy under the age of two in Bethlehem should be killed. He wasn't taking any chances!

But no sooner had the wise men left Bethlehem than an angel appeared to Joseph in a dream. "You must take Mary and Jesus and set off at once for Egypt," warned the angel. "You are in danger here, for Herod will be sending soldiers to search for the child and to kill him."

Joseph awoke with a start. He and Mary swiftly gathered their belongings, lifted little Jesus gently from his sleep, and set off in haste that very night on the long journey to Egypt, where they lived until wicked King Herod died. Then they came back to Nazareth once more, and as the years passed, Jesus grew to be filled with grace and wisdom and kindness.

Cousin John

Now, shortly before Jesus came into the world, another special baby was born. His name was John, and his parents were Zechariah and Elizabeth, who was Mary's cousin. Elizabeth and Zechariah were very old when John was born, so he was a wonderful gift from God, and God had a very special plan for him, for John was to prepare the way for Jesus.

When John grew up, he went to live in the desert. He wore clothes made of smelly camels' hair and lived on dry, crunchy locusts and wild honey! To be honest, he was rather strange, but nevertheless, people came from all around to listen to what he had to say, for his words rang true. "Be sorry for your sins, and God will forgive you. And get ready in your hearts, for your King is coming soon!" John would tell them. It wasn't enough for them to carry on the way they were—they needed to repent and change their ways. Many truly were sorry, and if they were, John took them down to the River Jordan, and there he baptized them in the water as a sign that all their sins had been washed away and that they could start a new life.

People began to wonder if maybe John was the one that the prophets had spoken about so many years ago, the promised King, but he told them, "I'm baptizing you with water, but the one who will come after me will baptize you with the Holy Spirit and with fire! I'm not even worthy to tie up his sandals!"

One day, John was by the river when Jesus came to him. As soon as he saw him, John knew who this special person was. Here was the holy "Lamb of God"! This made him all the more shocked when Jesus asked John to baptize him!

"You can't be serious!" he protested uncomfortably. "I shouldn't be baptizing you—I should be begging you to baptize me!"

But Jesus just smiled and told him that this was what God wanted, and so John took him into the river.

At the very moment that Jesus came up out of the water, the heavens opened and the skies shone brightly, and like a dove, the Holy Spirit rested on Jesus. Then a voice came from above, "This is my Son, and I love him. I am very pleased with him."

At last, the much longed-for King had come to save his people!

The Big Test

It was nearly time for Jesus to start spreading God's message to his people, but first of all, there was something he had to do.

The Holy Spirit led Jesus into the desert. It was dusty and stony and dry, and it was baking hot during the day. For forty days Jesus stayed in the desert, and in all that time he ate no food. Can you imagine that? By the end of that time he was very hungry indeed!

Then the devil came to test him—just as he had tested Adam and Eve in the Garden of Eden so many, many years before—saying, "If you're really the Son of God, surely you can do anything. Why don't you just tell these stones to become bread? How hard would that be?"

Jesus wasn't Adam. He answered calmly, "It says in the Scriptures, 'Man shall not live on bread alone, but on every word that comes from the mouth of God.'"

He knew that food wasn't the most important thing in life.

Not to be put off, the devil took Jesus to the top of a temple and told him to throw himself off. "If you're the Son of God, surely his angels would rescue you?" he taunted.

But Jesus said, "It is also written: 'Do not put the Lord your God to the test.'"

The devil tried yet again to tempt Jesus. He took him to the very top of a high mountain and showed him the land that stretched for miles and miles in every direction. "All you have to do is bow down and worship me, and I will give you all the kingdoms of the world!" he coaxed.

But Jesus replied, "Go away, Satan! For it is written: 'Worship the Lord your God, and serve only him.'"

When the devil finally realized that he could not tempt Jesus, he gave up in disgust and left him there in the desert, and God sent his angels to Jesus to help him recover.

Now it was time for Jesus to truly start his work on earth.

Jesus' Special Friends

Simon sat on the gently swaying boat, looking up at the man who stood talking by his side, and beyond him to the crowd of people on the shore, listening eagerly to what he had to say.

Today had not been like any other day. Simon had been mending his nets by the shore when a man had come to the lake and had begun speaking. Slowly but surely the crowds had gathered to listen to this man—Jesus, he was called—talk about God's love and forgiveness and explain the Scriptures in a way that seemed so different from the way the priests talked in the synagogues. When Jesus spoke, everything seemed clear.

But so many people came to listen that it was difficult for everyone to hear what Jesus was saying, and so Jesus had turned to Simon and had asked him if he wouldn't mind taking him out on his fishing boat so that people could see him more clearly. And now, along with the crowd, Simon drank in every word he had to say.

35

Afterwards, when the crowd had dispersed, Jesus told Simon to push the boat out farther into the water and let down his nets. "Master," Simon answered, "we were out all night and didn't catch a thing. But if you say so, then we will try again."

He couldn't believe his eyes when he pulled up his nets full of fish! He called to his brother, Andrew, and to his friends James and John to help, and soon the two boats were so full of fish that they were nearly ready to sink!

Simon fell to his knees in wonder, but Jesus smiled. "Don't be afraid, Simon. From now on you shall be called Peter (the Greek word for 'rock') for that is what you will be."

Then Jesus turned to all the men. "I want you to leave your nets," he said, "and come with me and fish for men instead so that we can spread the good news!"

The four men had been fishermen all their life—nets and tides, fish and sails were all they knew—yet they pulled their boats up on the beach, left everything behind, and followed Jesus without a backward glance!

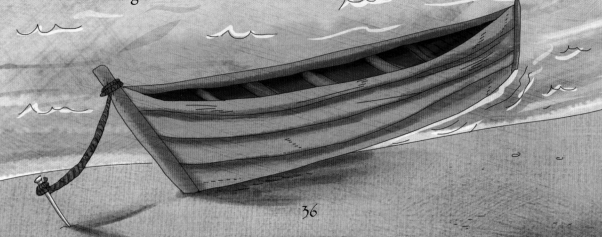

These were the first special friends that Jesus called to help him in his work, but they weren't the last. Over time, Jesus chose twelve men to be his disciples, to pass on his message of good news, and to be there, after his death, to carry on his work. They weren't all fishermen—there was also a tax collector, Matthew, who left his job on the spot when Jesus told him to follow him. Not everybody was thrilled when Jesus became friendly with Matthew, for people thought that tax collectors were greedy and dishonest. But Jesus told them, "If you go to a doctor's office, you don't expect to see healthy people—it's people who are sick who need to see the doctor. I am God's doctor. I have come here to save those people who are sinners and who want to start afresh. Those who have done nothing wrong don't need me!"

As well as the fishermen and Matthew, Jesus called another Simon, a patriot who wanted to fight the Romans, and six more men: Bartholomew, Thomas, James son of Alphaeus, Philip, Judas (or Thaddeus) son of James, and Judas Iscariot.

Jesus knew they would have a hard task ahead of them. He wanted them to teach the people that God's kingdom is near and to heal people too. Later on, these men became known as apostles, or messengers, for they were chosen especially by Jesus to pass on his message of good news.

Water into Wine

Not long after Jesus had called Simon Peter and the other fishermen to follow him, he was invited to a marvelous wedding party along with his friends and his mother. Everyone was having a wonderful time—the music was cheerful, the food was delicious, and the wine was… actually, everything was going well until the wine ran out!

Mary rushed to tell Jesus, who asked her, "Why are you telling me this? It is not yet time for me to show myself." But Mary still hoped he would help and spoke quietly to the servants, telling them to do whatever Jesus told them to.

There were several huge water jars nearby. Jesus told the servants to fill them with water and then pour the water into jugs and take it to the headwaiter to taste. When the headwaiter tasted it, he was amazed. He exclaimed to the bridegroom, "Most people serve the best wine at the start of a meal, but you have saved the best till last!" for the jugs were now filled with delicious wine!

This was the first of many miracles that Jesus would perform.

41

The Healer

Jesus traveled from town to town with his friends, spreading his message. One day he was walking through a village when a man came up to him and fell to his knees in front of him. "Sir," he begged, looking humbly up at Jesus, "If you want to, you can make me clean."

The people around Jesus edged back in fear and disgust. The man in front of them was a leper—he was suffering from a dreadful skin disease and was wrapped in bandages. He even smelled! Worse than that, they were worried that they might catch the disease too.

But Jesus was filled with compassion. He reached out and touched the man gently. "I do want to," he said. "Be clean!"

And no sooner had he spoken than the man's skin was smooth and clear and healthy, and people could hardly believe their eyes.

Jesus said to the man, "Don't tell anyone about this. Go straight to the priest and let him examine you."

But the grateful man simply couldn't keep the wonderful event to himself, and before long so many people wanted to come and see Jesus that he could no longer go anywhere without being surrounded by crowds. Now wherever Jesus went, people would flock to see him, not just to listen to all the amazing things he had to tell them but also for healing—for themselves or for their friends and family.

One time, some men brought their friend to the house where Jesus was staying. They hoped Jesus would heal him. Their friend was paralyzed and couldn't walk, so they carried him between them on a makeshift stretcher. When they got there, the house was so crowded they couldn't get in—they couldn't even get close to the front door! But the men weren't going to give up that easily. Instead, they climbed up onto the roof, made a hole in it, and then lowered the man down through the hole on a mat!

When Jesus saw how strongly they believed in him, he spoke kindly to the man, saying, "Your sins are forgiven, my friend." Jesus knew what was truly important.

But among the people inside the house were several teachers of the law. They were very offended when they heard Jesus say this. This was outrageous! Who did he think he was? Only God could forgive sin!

Jesus knew exactly what they were thinking. He turned to them and said calmly, "Do you think it's easier to say to this man, 'Your sins are forgiven,' or to say, 'Get up and walk'? The Son of Man has authority on earth to forgive sins."

Then he turned back to the man and said, "Get up now. Pick up your mat and go home," and the man stood up, picked up the mat, and walked straight out the front door! Everyone was filled with wonder.

45

The Sermon on the Mount

For many people, the words that Jesus spoke healed them deep within. More and more people wanted to listen to this wonderful man—but the priests and teachers of the law weren't always so pleased to have him around. They felt that he was stepping on their toes and saying things that he had no right to say. They wanted people to listen to them, not him! All too often, Jesus wasn't made welcome in the synagogues, so sometimes he would teach his disciples and the large crowds that gathered to hear him outside in the open air. One of the most important talks he gave was on a mountain near Capernaum. It has become known as the Sermon on the Mount. Jesus taught the people about what was truly important in life and gave them comfort and advice on how to live their lives.

He told them, "It is important to obey all of God's laws, but that isn't enough—you need to understand the meaning behind them. You need to learn to truly forgive people when they do something you don't like or that hurts you. That is the way to get closer to God. It's easy to love those who love you, but I say, love your enemies! After all, God gives his sunlight and rain to both good and bad people!"

He told them that they should try to set a good example to others—"but don't just do good things in order to impress other people. You don't need anyone else's praise—God can see inside your hearts, and he knows the truth! And always try to treat other people in the same way that you would like them to treat you. Don't judge them. Think about your own faults first!"

He offered them comfort as well. He told them that all those who were poor or sad, or who had lived a hard life, would one day be happy in heaven. So too would all those who were kind and humble, all those who kept the peace and who tried to do the right thing. They would all be rewarded in heaven, so they must not give up hope, however hard things seemed.

"That is what you need to focus on—the end goal," he continued. "Don't store up wealth on earth. It won't last! Store up treasures in heaven, for where your treasures are, your heart will be too. Don't worry about what clothes you're wearing or where your next meal will come from. There is more to life than food and clothes. Look at the birds in the sky. They don't have to plant and harvest and store their food, but God feeds them, doesn't he?

"And what about the beautiful wildflowers that grow everywhere? They don't have to work hard either, for God himself clothes them, and how splendid they look dressed in all their wonderful colors! And if God cares for the birds and the flowers, don't you think he loves you even more? So trust him to look after you!"

Jesus also taught people the right way to pray. They shouldn't try to impress others by praying in public, but should go to a quiet place and pray to God alone. Nor should they keep repeating meaningless words. God knows what is in our hearts, and this is the way Jesus told people to pray to him:

Our Father in heaven,
Hallowed be your name.
Your kingdom come.
Your will be done,
on earth as it is in heaven.
Give us today our daily bread,
and forgive us our sins,
as we forgive those who sin against us.
Lead us not into temptation,
but deliver us from evil.
For yours is the kingdom,
the power and the glory, forever.
Amen.

"Keep on asking," said Jesus, "and you will receive. Keep on seeking, and you will find. Keep on knocking, and the door will be opened to you."

Before Jesus ended his sermon, he said one last thing: "If you listen to my teaching and follow it, you are wise, like the person who builds his house on solid rock. Even if the rain pours down, the rivers flood, and the winds rage, the house won't collapse because it is built on solid rock.

"But if you listen and don't obey, you are foolish, like a person who builds a house on sand, without any foundations. The house might be built very quickly, but when the rains and floods and winds come, the house won't be able to stand against them. It will collapse and be completely destroyed."

As the crowds slowly dispersed, their heads were filled with all these new ideas. Jesus was nothing like their usual teachers, but what he said made sense. They had a lot to think about!

The Man Who Amazed Jesus

One day, Jesus was in Capernaum. He spent a lot of his time in this small fishing town on the banks of the Sea of Galilee. This was where he had met Simon Peter and the others, and where Matthew used to collect taxes.

In Capernaum there lived a Roman officer. Romans didn't normally get on well with the Jews, but this officer was a good man who treated the Jews well. He was also kind to the people who worked for him in his house, and that was why, when he heard that Jesus was in Capernaum, he came to ask for his help, for one of his servants was very ill.

"Lord," the officer said to Jesus, "my servant is very sick. He can't get out of bed, and he is suffering awfully. I am ever so fond of him, but I'm afraid he is close to death."

Jesus asked him, "Shall I come and heal him?"

But the officer replied, "Lord, I don't deserve to have you come to my own house! I am not worthy of that! But I know that you don't need to anyway. If you just say the word, I know that my servant will be healed, just in the same way that when I order my soldiers to do something, they do it!" The officer believed in Jesus so completely that he didn't even need him to visit the sick man himself!

Jesus was amazed. He said to the people around him, "I've never come across faith like this before!" Then he turned back to the officer, saying, "Go home now, and what you believe will be done for you."

So the officer returned to his house, and sure enough, when he arrived back home, he found his servant up on his feet and feeling perfectly well again!

Jesus Calms the Storm

It was a beautiful evening. Peter and John and the other disciples were in a small fishing boat, heading happily over the Sea of Galilee. Jesus had spent all day by the lake, talking to people about God's message. People had come from far and wide to hear what he had to say and to listen to his wonderful stories about God's love and forgiveness, and now Jesus was tired out. In fact, the minute he had lain down in the boat, he had fallen fast asleep!

The waters were calm and peaceful, and small waves lapped against the side of the boat and ruffled the sails as the friends chatted quietly about the day's events. Suddenly, the skies above darkened as clouds rolled in above them. A fierce storm struck the lake, the wind howled angrily, and huge waves tossed the boat from side to side.

The friends jumped up to reef the sails but could hardly keep their footing as the boat lurched violently and water poured into the boat. Lightning lit up the dark sky, and thunder echoed overhead. Some of the disciples were fishermen. They had sailed on these waters all their lives—the Sea of Galilee was known for its sudden squalls and raging storms—but never had they seen a storm as terrible and as terrifying as this one! They could hardly hear themselves think for the roar of the wind and the hammering of the rain, and they feared that at any moment their small boat could capsize.

Yet through it all, Jesus slept peacefully in the stern!

"Master, Master!" cried the frightened disciples. "Wake up and save us!"

Jesus opened his eyes and looked up at them. "Why are you so afraid?" he said sadly. "You have so little faith!"

Then he stood up calmly in the swaying boat and turned to face the wind and driving rain. "Be still," he said. That was all, nothing more. Just, "Be still."

And the storm was gone! The wind and the waves died down, the rain stopped, and everything was calm once more.

The friends looked at one another. Something far more shocking than the storm had just happened. Who was this man who could speak to the wind and the waves—and be obeyed! They did not yet understand the truth that this was truly the Son of God who would save them all.

So long as Jesus is with us, there is nothing to be afraid of. If he can calm the storms of the sea with just a couple of words, he can calm the storms of life as well.

Just Sleeping

Poor Jairus was in a dreadful state! His heart ached as he watched his wife wring her hands together in despair, for his little girl was terribly ill. She was only twelve years old and was the light of their life, and nothing that they did seemed to make any difference. The doctors had given up hope. But Jairus hadn't. He had learned that Jesus was in town, and he had heard the rumors about all the wonderful things he had done and all the people he had managed to cure. He was certain that all he needed to do was to get Jesus to come and see his daughter, and all would be well—but he knew he was running out of time!

When he found Jesus, surrounded by a multitude of people, he threw himself at his feet and begged him to come and help his little girl, for she was dying. Jesus helped Jairus to his feet and promised that he would come immediately.

But people crowded around on all sides, everyone eager to see Jesus and to get close to him. Jairus's heart was pounding. He was so worried that they wouldn't get there in time.

And then his heart sank, for Jesus stopped still. "Who touched me?" he asked, looking around him.

"Master, everyone is touching you in this crowd!" said a disciple, but Jesus knew that he had been touched in a special way.

As he looked around, a woman stepped forward hesitantly and knelt at his feet. "Lord, it was me," she said nervously. For years she had been ill, and nobody had been able to help her. But she had known that if she could just get close to Jesus, just touch him, she would be healed. And sure enough, the moment she had managed to touch the edge of his cloak, she was well again!

Jesus wasn't angry. "Your faith has made you well," he said kindly to the woman, smiling down at her. "Go home now and be at peace." And the woman left, full of gratitude and happiness.

But just then, someone came running up to Jairus. It was one of his servants. His face was grim, and Jairus didn't need to wait for him to speak to know that the news was bad. They were too late! Jairus's daughter was dead. Poor Jairus was heartbroken, but Jesus carried on walking. "Trust me, Jairus," he said. "Don't be afraid. Just believe."

When Jesus and Jairus arrived at the house, the air was filled with the sound of weeping. "Why are you carrying on so?" he asked. "The girl is not dead—she is just sleeping." The people there laughed at him bitterly, for they knew perfectly well that the child was dead. But Jesus ignored them and went into the house along with Peter and James and John, and Jairus and his wife. Everyone else he told to wait outside.

Then Jesus went to the room where the little girl lay on the bed, perfectly still. Tenderly taking one of her hands in his own, Jesus whispered, "Wake up, my child!"

In that instant, the child opened her eyes. She smiled at Jesus and hugged her overjoyed parents! Jesus told them to go and bring her some food, and he also told them not to talk about what had happened.

There is nothing that Jesus cannot do. Don't be afraid—just believe!

Special Stories

Many of the people who came to listen to Jesus were craftsmen or farmers, and many more kept animals or had their own vegetable garden. Jesus tried to pass on his message in a way that they would understand. He made up stories, often called parables, to let people think things through for themselves. To some they would just be stories, but others would understand the real message . . .

"A farmer went out to sow some seeds," said Jesus, looking at the bright and eager faces all around him. "As he was scattering it, some fell along the path and was trampled on or eaten by birds. Some fell on rocky ground where there was no soil, and when those seeds began to grow into little plants, they withered up and died because their roots couldn't reach water. Other seeds fell among weeds, which wrapped round them and choked them. But some seeds—a few—fell on good soil and grew into tall, strong, healthy plants and produced a wonderful crop, far greater than what was sown."

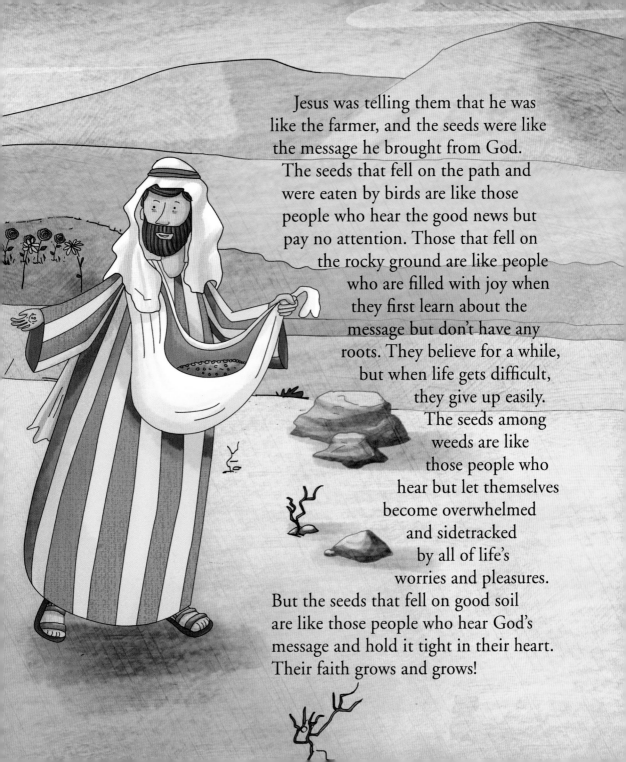

Jesus was telling them that he was like the farmer, and the seeds were like the message he brought from God. The seeds that fell on the path and were eaten by birds are like those people who hear the good news but pay no attention. Those that fell on the rocky ground are like people who are filled with joy when they first learn about the message but don't have any roots. They believe for a while, but when life gets difficult, they give up easily. The seeds among weeds are like those people who hear but let themselves become overwhelmed and sidetracked by all of life's worries and pleasures. But the seeds that fell on good soil are like those people who hear God's message and hold it tight in their heart. Their faith grows and grows!

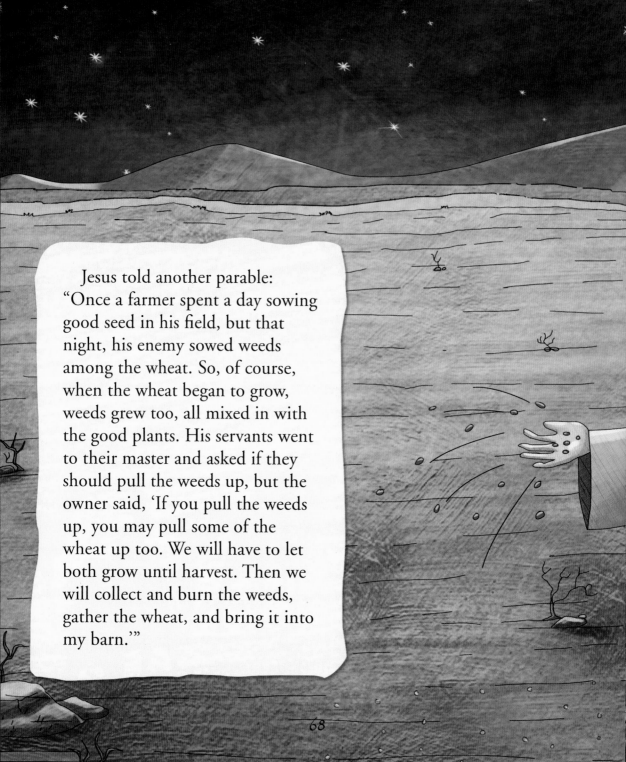

Jesus told another parable: "Once a farmer spent a day sowing good seed in his field, but that night, his enemy sowed weeds among the wheat. So, of course, when the wheat began to grow, weeds grew too, all mixed in with the good plants. His servants went to their master and asked if they should pull the weeds up, but the owner said, 'If you pull the weeds up, you may pull some of the wheat up too. We will have to let both grow until harvest. Then we will collect and burn the weeds, gather the wheat, and bring it into my barn.'"

Later on that evening, the disciples asked Jesus what the story meant. Jesus explained, "The farmer who sowed the good seed is the Son of Man. The field is the world, and the good seed is the people of the kingdom. The weeds were sown by the devil, and they are his people. The harvest will come at the end of time. Then the Son of Man will send out his angels, and they will weed out of his kingdom everything that causes sin and all those people who do evil things and think evil thoughts and throw them into the blazing furnace. But those people who are good will shine as brightly as the sun in the kingdom of their Father."

If you have a vegetable garden, however carefully you look after it, and however many carrots and potatoes and peas and tomatoes you grow in it, there are probably some nasty weeds too. If we try to dig them out, we might dig out some of the good plants too. If we try to use weed killer on them—well, most weed killers don't know the difference between one plant and the next and will just kill everything! So sometimes, it is best to wait until harvest time, and then you can pull up and enjoy all your wonderful fruit and vegetables and throw the weeds on the bonfire!

In life, we can come across people who are like weeds in a garden. But it isn't our job to judge them—leave the weeds for God to take care of, and try to show love and kindness to all of his people.

The Mustard Seed and the Yeast

Jesus told his followers another parable: "The kingdom of heaven is like a mustard seed, which a man took and planted in the ground. Now, a mustard seed is tiny—in fact, it's the smallest of all seeds, but don't let that fool you because when it grows, it can grow bigger than all the other herbs and become a tree big enough that the birds can come and perch in its branches!"

Then he continued, "The kingdom of heaven is like yeast that a woman took and mixed into about sixty pounds of flour until it worked all through the dough." You see, you only need a very small amount of yeast to add to some flour and water and a bit of salt and sugar to make a lovely big loaf of bread. Sixty pounds of flour is quite a lot of flour, but you don't need lots of yeast. Just a small piece of yeast will have a huge effect.

Jesus was saying that we are never too small to be important in God's eyes and that however little we are, we can help to grow the kingdom of God. From small beginnings can come wonderful things!

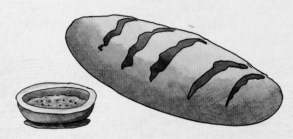

Hidden Treasure

Jesus was speaking to his disciples. Everyone else had gone home, but he had a special message for his friends: "The kingdom of heaven is like treasure hidden in a field," he told them. "Once there was a man who was digging in a field. He came upon a chest of buried treasure! When he opened it, it was full of gold coins and wonderful jewels that sparkled and shone in the sunlight. The man was so excited that he put the chest back in the ground and covered it up carefully with soil. Then he rushed off and sold his house and his land and everything he had just so that he could buy that field and own the treasure himself!"

Jesus continued, "The kingdom of heaven is like a merchant on the lookout for beautiful pearls. He would travel the countryside in search of pearls. One day he came across one more beautiful than he had ever seen before. It was perfect! The merchant thought it was so precious that he sold everything he had so that he could buy this one pearl."

Jesus was talking about the most important thing of all—God's love. This love is the greatest treasure that we can possibly find. It is more precious than silver or gold or jewels—and absolutely worth giving everything else up for!

A Lamp on a Stand

Jesus wanted to explain how important it was for his followers to hear his message, take it to heart, and then pass it on. He said to them, "No one lights a lamp and then covers it up with a bowl or hides it under a bed. Instead, they put the lamp on a stand so that anyone who comes in will see the light. Everything that is hidden will become clear, and everything that is secret will be brought out into the open."

He wanted them to think very carefully about what he was telling them so that they themselves could be lamps, shining forth in the world, bringing light into the lives of those around them. A light is made to be seen and to be used—we must use what God has given us!

They weren't to keep his wonderful news a secret for themselves. They should share it, and in doing so would be filled with light. Jesus is the light of the world, and he came into it, not to stay hidden, but to light up the world with the truth about God. And when we let Jesus into our hearts, we shine too!

Five Loaves of Bread and Two Fish

News about Jesus and the wonderful stories that he told and things that he did spread throughout the land. Everywhere Jesus went he was surrounded by people.

One day, Jesus and his disciples had sailed across the lake to a quiet, remote place, away from the towns and cities, to spend some time alone. But the crowds had followed Jesus even there, and he could not bring himself to send them away, for they were like sheep without a shepherd, and his heart was filled with love and pity for them.

He spent all day talking, his words helping to set these people on the path toward his Father in heaven, and when evening fell the crowds were still there—about five thousand of them! No one seemed to want to go home!

The disciples gathered around Jesus. "Master," said one, "what shall we do? Shouldn't we send these people off to find food for themselves? It's getting very late!"

"They don't need to go away," said Jesus. "Give them something to eat yourselves."

"But Master!" exclaimed the disciples, "we don't have any food to give them, and it would cost a fortune to go and buy food for them all!"

"What food do we have?" asked Jesus calmly, and after a frantic scrabbling around, the disciples came up with five loaves of bread and a couple of fish that one little boy happened to have for his dinner. Five loaves of bread and two fish—for five thousand people!

The disciples were rather bewildered, but Jesus simply told them to get the people to sit down on the grass in groups, and then he took the loaves of bread and the two fish, looked up to heaven and gave thanks to his Father, and broke the loaves into pieces. He gave them to the disciples, who put them in baskets and took them to the people and then came back to Jesus for more bread and fish. He filled up their baskets again…and again…and again! To their astonishment there was still bread and fish left in the baskets when they came to feed the very last people! More than five thousand people had been fed that day—with five loaves of bread and two fish!

You see, even when we don't have very much, if we give what we have to God and trust in him, he can do more with it than we could ever have imagined!

Walking on Water

It was late at night. All the crowds had finally gone home, and now the disciples were on their own in a fishing boat in the middle of the lake. Jesus had sent them on ahead of him to travel over to the other side of the lake while he stayed behind to be alone and to pray on a quiet hillside.

But the disciples were worried. A sudden squall had come upon them. The wind howled furiously, and waves tossed the boat violently. They rowed as hard as they could, but they didn't seem to be getting anywhere fast. At the first light of dawn, they saw a figure walking toward them on the water! They were overcome with fear—was it a ghost? But then they heard the calm voice of Jesus saying, "It is I. Don't be afraid."

Simon Peter was the first to speak. "Lord," he said, "if it is really you, then order me to walk across the water to you." Jesus answered Simon Peter and said, "Come."

Simon Peter put one foot gingerly in the water. Then he lowered the other and bravely stood up, letting go of the boat. He didn't sink! But when he looked around at the waves, his courage failed him. As he began to sink, he cried out, "Lord, save me!"

Jesus reached out and took his hand. "Oh, Peter," he said sadly, "where is your faith? Why did you doubt?"

Then together they walked back to the boat. The wind died down, and the water became calm. The disciples bowed low. They were filled with awe and wonder. "You really are the Son of God!" they said humbly.

In our lives we will go through many storms. Keep your eyes on Jesus, and you will be safe.

On the Mountaintop

Jesus climbed up a mountain to pray, taking with him Peter, James, and John. It was a wonderful place to stop and think in peace and quiet and to see things clearly.

All of a sudden, as Jesus prayed, the disciples looked up to see him changed. Light shone from his face, and his clothes became whiter than anyone could wash them, dazzlingly white! As they watched in wonder, Moses, who had led his people out of Egypt, and Elijah, greatest of all the prophets, were suddenly there before their very eyes, talking with Jesus! Then a bright cloud covered them, and a voice said, "This is my own dear Son, whom I love. Listen to what he has to say, for I am very pleased with him!"

The disciples fell to the ground, too frightened to raise their eyes. But Jesus came over and touched them. "Don't be afraid," he said softly, and when they looked up, they saw no one there except Jesus.

When Jesus was on earth, there were lots of different ideas about who he really was. Some people thought that he was another prophet or someone come back from the dead—Elijah, maybe, or John the Baptist, who had been killed by King Herod. Others just thought he was a good teacher, and there were probably plenty of people who just thought he was rather strange!

But from that moment on, Peter, James, and John had no doubt at all about who Jesus was. He was the Son of God. God had said it, and that was that.

The Frantic Father

The very next day, when Jesus and his friends came down from the mountain, the other disciples came to meet them. They were surrounded by a large crowd, and out of the crowd a man called out in anguish, "Teacher, please look at my son! He is possessed by a demon, and he has dreadful fits. Sometimes he can't speak, or he is thrown to the ground and foams at the mouth! Please, please help him! I asked your disciples to help, but they couldn't drive the demon out."

Jesus looked at the disciples in disappointment. "Why don't you people believe? How long must I put up with you?" he said in sorrow. His disciples had seen so much and had done so much, and yet they still didn't have the faith to heal this boy and cast out the bad spirit.

He told them to bring the young boy to him, and as soon as the boy came close to Jesus, the spirit threw the child to the ground, where he rolled around, foaming at the mouth uncontrollably.

"If you can really do anything, please help us!" begged the father.

"'If you can?'" repeated Jesus. "'*If?*' Don't you know that anything is possible for someone who truly believes?"

The father exclaimed, "I do believe! Help me believe more!"

Then Jesus commanded the spirit to come out, and the boy was healed. As simple as that!

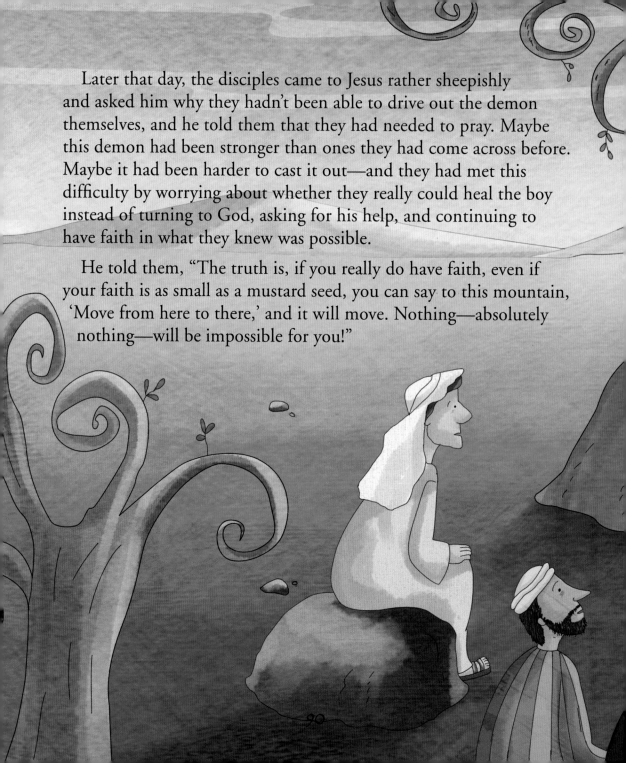

Later that day, the disciples came to Jesus rather sheepishly and asked him why they hadn't been able to drive out the demon themselves, and he told them that they had needed to pray. Maybe this demon had been stronger than ones they had come across before. Maybe it had been harder to cast it out—and they had met this difficulty by worrying about whether they really could heal the boy instead of turning to God, asking for his help, and continuing to have faith in what they knew was possible.

He told them, "The truth is, if you really do have faith, even if your faith is as small as a mustard seed, you can say to this mountain, 'Move from here to there,' and it will move. Nothing—absolutely nothing—will be impossible for you!"

The Good Neighbor

Once a lawyer asked Jesus a question. He wanted to know what Jesus thought he should do to be able to live forever in heaven. Jesus turned the question back on the man. "What do you think you should do?" he asked. "What does the law say?"

"'Love God with all your heart and all your soul,' and 'Love your neighbor just as you love yourself,'" replied the man rather smugly. After all, he was an expert in the law!

Jesus nodded. "You're right. If you do this, you will inherit eternal life." But he knew the man hadn't finished yet. He waited.

"So who exactly *is* my neighbor?" the lawyer continued. "Is it the couple who live in the next house to mine or the people farther down the road?"

Jesus looked around at all the people. This was a very important thing to ask. When God had given Moses the special commandments so long ago, there had been two commandments which were more important than all the rest—"Love God with all your heart, and all your soul, and all your strength, and all your mind," and "Love your neighbor just as you love yourself,"—just as the lawyer had said. These commandments were so very important because if people truly loved God and truly loved other people, they would want to follow all the other commandments anyway.

But the man in the crowd had missed the point. Jesus wanted to explain just what God meant.

"Once there was a man who was traveling from Jerusalem to Jericho," Jesus began. The people who had gathered around him made themselves comfortable—Jesus was clearly going to tell one of his special stories!

"This man," continued Jesus, "was walking along the dusty road when all of a sudden some men jumped out from behind some rocks and began hitting him. They pushed him to the ground and kicked him and then stole everything he had with him—his bag, his money, and even his clothes. They left him there in a ditch by the roadside and ran away into the hills.

"The poor man lay bleeding by the side of the road, barely able to lift his head. After a while, a priest came by. Now, the priest saw the beaten man, but he looked away and turned his horse toward the other side of the road, as far away from him as he could get. He carried on his way without one further glance.

"Time passed, and then another man came walking along the road. This man was a Levite who worked in the temple in Jerusalem. But he, too, turned his face the other way and quickly walked by without stopping.

"Then, along the road came a Samaritan." (Now, the Jews and the Samaritans didn't get along at all, so no one would have expected a Samaritan to stop for a Jew.)

"But this traveler did not see his enemy by the roadside—he saw a poor injured man who needed help. He felt so sorry for him. He knelt down on the ground beside him and carefully washed and bandaged his wounds. Then he helped him onto the back of his donkey and took him to an inn. He even gave the innkeeper money to look after the man until he was well."

Jesus looked at the man who had asked him the question in the first place. "So," he asked, "who do *you* think was a good neighbor to the injured man?"

The man sheepishly replied, "The one who was kind to him."

Then Jesus told him, "Then go and be like him."

Being a good neighbor to someone isn't about where they live or where you live, or whether they come from the same sort of family as you or even the same country as you. It is about showing God's wonderful love to all those in need, whoever they are and wherever they may be.

The Rich Fool

Jesus wanted to warn his followers to be on their guard against all kinds of greed. Life shouldn't be about owning lots of things or making lots of money. He explained this to them in a parable:

"Once there was a rich man who owned a lot of land. One year he had a truly wonderful harvest. In fact, he had so many crops that he didn't have enough room to store them all! So he had an idea. He had plenty already, and he could have chosen to share the extra crops, but he didn't want to do that. Instead, he decided to knock down all his barns and build bigger and better ones so that he could store all his grain. That way he would have enough put aside for years, and he could spend his time enjoying himself with lots of good food and drink and generally taking life easy.

"But God said to him, 'You fool, this very night your life will be over, and who will have all this then?'"

The rich man couldn't take all his wealth with him after his death. His greed and selfishness would do him no good in the end.

Jesus was saying that we shouldn't spend our lives laying up treasure for ourselves. If God blesses us, we should use what he gives us to help others, and then we will be rich toward God.

99

Be Ready!

Jesus told his followers that they needed to be ready at all times for the day when he would come again. To help them understand what he meant, he told them a story about some good servants who were waiting for their master to return from a wedding feast. They didn't know when he would be back, for in those times wedding feasts could last for days—food, wine, music, dancing—there was no knowing when he might appear at the door! Nevertheless, the faithful servants stayed dressed and ready for action, and they kept the lamps cheerfully burning so that the instant he knocked upon the door, they could open it for him.

Jesus went on to say that the servants would be richly rewarded for their readiness, for when he came back, the master would be so pleased with them that he would put on an apron, sit them down at the table, and wait on them himself! This is how Jesus will reward us if he returns to find us ready for him.

But things won't be so pleasant for those who are unprepared and who are sleepwalking their way through life. Those people will be like the bad servant who loses patience while waiting for his master's return, and starts being mean to the other servants, and helps himself to food and too much drink. When the master comes back unexpectedly, he will be very angry, and the servant will surely be punished!

So let us be ready, for if we are not prepared when Jesus comes, there will be no time to get ready then. Let him instead find us watching, waiting, and serving God as best we can.

The Wise and Foolish Girls

Jesus told his followers another story to help them understand that they must be ready at all times for his return, for they would never know when it might happen.

"Once ten girls were waiting to join a wedding feast. They didn't know how long it would be before the bridegroom would turn up, and so they all brought lamps with them, but only five of the girls thought to bring some spare oil with them. The other five brought their lamps but didn't have any spare oil.

"They were excited and chattered happily among themselves, but time passed by and the bridegroom didn't come, and one by one, the tired girls fell asleep.

"Suddenly, at midnight, a cry rang out, for the bridegroom was coming, and the girls woke up with a start. They rushed to light their lamps, but those of the foolish girls soon began to flicker, for their oil had run out.

103

"The foolish girls turned to the other girls and begged them to spare them some of their oil, but the wise girls replied, 'No, there isn't enough for all of us. You'll have to go and buy some more!' And the wise girls went off to join the bridegroom and went in with him to the feast.

"By the time the foolish girls returned with lighted lamps, the door was shut, and though they knocked loudly, they were told, 'You are too late. I don't know who you are!'"

Jesus told his disciples, "Always be ready, because you don't know the day or the hour of my return!"

What must we do to be prepared? Invite Jesus to come into our hearts!

The Useless Fig Tree

Jesus once told a story about a man who had a fig tree in his vineyard. One day, the man went to look at it, hoping to find some fruit, and was disappointed to see that there was none on it. He went and found the gardener and said to him, "Look, I've been coming to check on this tree for three years now, and it hasn't produced a single fig! What's going on? I really think it's about time you cut it down! It's using up precious soil for nothing."

But the gardener pleaded with his master to leave the tree for one more year to see if it would bear fruit. "Master," he said, "why don't I dig up the soil all around the tree. And I'll pop in some fertilizer too. Let's give it another year, and if it still isn't producing any fruit then, I promise I will cut it down." His master agreed.

Many people believe that in this parable Jesus was referring to the nation of Israel, who had lost their way. But the message is for all of us even today: God is the owner of the vineyard, and Jesus is his gardener. Jesus has come to plead for more time for us to bear fruit—and, more than that, he is prepared to help us by tending the soil around us! Let's make the most of his tender care and bear fruit for him.

The Great Banquet

"Once," said Jesus, "there was a king who was planning on holding a great feast. It was to be a very special occasion because it was to celebrate his son's wedding. The excited king spent days planning it and inviting all the people that he wanted to share the occasion with.

"At last, it was time. The table was laid, and the food was ready. The king sent his servants off to tell the guests that it was time to come. You would have thought that they would have been thrilled to have been invited to such a nice meal, but every last one of them had some kind of excuse—they were busy with work, they had to feed the animals, their wife was sick, and so on and so forth. Not one of them bothered to stop what they were doing and come to the feast—and some of them were even rude and nasty to the servants!

"When the king heard this, he was furious. 'They don't deserve to come!' he told his servants in disgust. 'Go back outside, and this time go and invite all the poor people, anyone who is blind or crippled or lame, and bring them in to enjoy the banquet!'

"And when this had been done, and there were still some empty places at the table, the king told his servants to search even farther, find yet more people, and make them come in so that his house would be full. As for the original, ungrateful guests who couldn't be bothered to turn up, the king vowed that not a single one of them would get even a taste of his feast!

"And what a wonderful feast it was! The tables were creaking under the weight of all the tasty dishes and delicious things to eat, and there were jugs and jugs of the very best wine. Everyone had a lovely time!"

God had invited his people to be saved through his Son, Jesus Christ, but many of them, especially the Pharisees and the teachers of the law, had refused to accept Jesus as their Savior—they had made all kind of excuses to explain why he wasn't the Son of God and had taken refuge in all their laws and traditions. So God extended his invitation all across the world—to everybody, not just the Jews.

God has invited us all to his wonderful feast—let's not miss out!

"I Forgive You
(Seventy-Seven Times)!"

Jesus tried to make his followers understand how important forgiveness was. Once Peter asked him, "Lord, how many times should I forgive someone who has done something bad to me? Up to seven times?"

Jesus looked him straight in the eyes. "Don't just forgive him seven times, Peter. Forgive him seventy-seven times!" he answered. This was important, so he told one of his special stories so that those listening could think about it very carefully.

"The kingdom of heaven," said Jesus as people stopped what they were doing to listen, and made themselves comfortable, "is like the master whose servant owed him a great deal of money. Not just a little—a lot! When it came time to pay it back, the man didn't have enough money. He was really worried about what his master would do, so he came to see him. He was trembling and nervously begged him for some more time.

"The kind master didn't give him more time—no, he canceled the debt altogether! 'Go home to your family,' he said, 'and forget about the money!'

"So the servant rushed home to tell his wife the wonderful news!

"Now, this very same servant was owed a small amount of money by another one of the servants in the household. He went to find the other man and grabbed him round the neck, shouting, 'Give me the money you owe me!'

"When the man admitted that he didn't have enough money to pay him back right then, the first servant was furious with him. So furious, in fact, that he didn't offer him any more time to find the money, but instead made sure that he was thrown into prison then and there!

"It wasn't long before the master of the household found out what had been going on. He called the first servant in to see him. 'What have you done?' the master asked in disgust. 'I canceled your debt to me because you begged me to. I would have thought you would have shown the same kindness to this other man as I showed to you—but no, you have been cruel and unkind, and I am really disappointed in you!' The master was so angry that he handed the servant over to the jailers until he could pay back all he owed."

Jesus looked at his followers. "This is how my Father will treat you unless you forgive your brother or sister from your heart."

Just as God forgives us over and over again, Jesus taught us that we need to forgive those around us—over and over again.

Lost and Found

The Pharisees and the teachers of the law got rather upset when Jesus hung out with the wrong sort of people. They muttered among themselves when they saw Jesus mixing with tax collectors and with people who had done bad things. They didn't really seem to understand what Jesus was trying to say about forgiveness. He tried to get them to see that there will be far more rejoicing in heaven over the one sinner who repents than over the ninety-nine good people who don't need to repent.

He said to them, "Imagine you had a hundred sheep and lost one of them. How would you feel? Wouldn't you leave the other ninety-nine safe and sound, and rush off to look for the lost one? Don't you think you would search high and low, in the wind or the rain or the snow, and keep on searching until you found it? And when you did find it, don't you think you would be so thrilled that you would rush home and celebrate?

"Or picture a woman," continued Jesus, "who had ten silver coins and who lost one of those precious coins. Wouldn't she light a lamp? Don't you think she would take a brush and sweep every single corner of the room and search every nook and cranny until she found it? And when she did find it, how happy and relieved would she be? Don't you think she would get all her friends and neighbors together and tell them about the lost coin and how she had found it, and ask them to be happy for her?"

God cares about each and every one of us. He loves all the people who believe in him and try to live in the way he teaches. But that isn't enough. No, we are all so important to him that he will try to save every last one of us.

The Lost Son

Jesus told another story to explain how God loves to forgive us and how happy God is when sinners admit that they are wrong and return to him.

"Once there was a man who had two sons," began Jesus. "One day, the youngest son came to his father and asked him if he could have the money that he would inherit after his father died. He wanted the money now because he longed to go traveling and exploring and do lots of fun things and be his own boss. He didn't want to stay at home on the farm. It was too boring!

"The father was sad, but he gave his son the money without any argument and sent him on his way with a sigh.

"At first, the young man had a marvelous time. He went to some wonderful places, met some interesting people, and basically did whatever he wanted, whenever he wanted. He had plenty of money, so he could buy anything that took his fancy. Life was fun!"

Jesus' listeners looked at one another. Things seemed to be working out fine for the young man—what was the problem? He had everything he wanted, didn't he?

But Jesus hadn't finished. That wasn't the end of the story…

"Time went on," continued Jesus, "and the young man spent more and more of his money enjoying himself. Soon, all the money was gone. Every last penny! Now things weren't so much fun! The young man had no choice but to look for work, for he had no money for a place to stay or even for food. Finally, he ended up working for a pig farmer. All day long he looked after the pigs, cleaning out the mucky pigsty and giving them food. He was so hungry that he found himself looking at the scraps he was giving to the animals and wishing he could eat it himself!

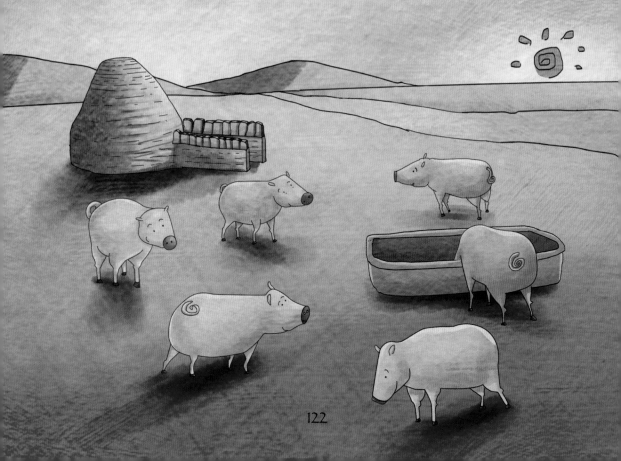

"At last he thought, 'This is ridiculous! My father feeds his servants better than this!' and he decided to go home and tell him how sorry he was and how silly he had been. 'I'm not worthy of being his son,' he thought to himself, 'but maybe he will let me work on the farm.'

123

"When his father saw him coming along the road, he rushed out and threw his arms around him. The young man tried to tell him that he was not fit to be called his son, but his father shushed him and told him not to speak nonsense. Then he called his servants to him and told them to bring his finest robe for his son to wear and to kill the prize calf for a wonderful feast.

"Not everyone was quite so thrilled. In fact, the older son was furious! He felt that he had worked hard for his father all this time, and nobody had ever held a feast for him! Yet now, here came his brother waltzing in, having squandered all his money, and his father couldn't wait to kill the fattened calf and welcome him home!

"'My son,' the father said to him patiently, 'you are always with me, and all I have is yours. But celebrate with me now, for your brother was dead to me and is alive again; he was lost and is found!'"

Like the boy in the story, we don't always make the right choices. Sometimes we make mistakes and do silly things. But isn't it good to know that God is always ready and willing to forgive us and to welcome us home with open arms?

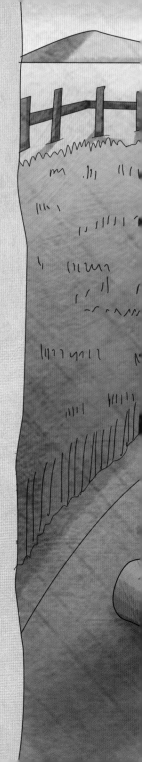

The Rich Man and the Beggar

Once Jesus told a story about two very different men who led very different lives. "There was once a rich man," began Jesus, "who lived a life of luxury. He lived in a grand house, and wore fine clothes, and had lots of servants. Every day his dining table was covered from end to end with delicious plates of food. Every day was a feast!

"Now, just outside the gates to his house you would find a poor, hungry beggar named Lazarus, whose skin was covered with sores. He sat on the roadside day after day, hoping desperately for a scrap of food or a coin from whoever walked by. Lazarus had nowhere to live, and he had hardly anything to eat. As he sat outside the rich man's house, the enticing smells of the rich man's food would waft past his nose to torment him as his empty stomach rumbled with hunger. How he longed for even the crumbs that fell from the rich man's table! How happy he would have been with just their leftovers. But the rich man was selfish and never stopped to think about poor Lazarus. In fact, Lazarus been sitting outside his gate for so long that he hardly even noticed him anymore.

"At last Lazarus's suffering was over, for he died and the angels carried him up to heaven to Abraham, where he felt no more pain or cold or hunger.

"Some time after, the rich man also died, but when he passed away no angels came for him. Instead, he was sent to the place for wicked people, for he had been mean and selfish. In torment, he looked up to heaven and begged, 'Father Abraham, please take pity on me and send Lazarus to dip his finger in water and cool my tongue, for I'm so thirsty!'

"But Abraham replied, 'Did you take pity on Lazarus? Did you give him food when he was hungry? You had a great time on earth, while Lazarus was suffering, but now he is looked after up here, and it is your turn to suffer.'

"'Then please, Father Abraham,' pleaded the rich man, 'at least warn my brothers before it is too late, so that they don't make the same mistakes that I did!'

"'Oh, son,' said Abraham, shaking his head sadly, 'they already have the writings of Moses and the prophets to warn them. It's their own fault if they don't change their ways in time to avoid the same fate as you!'"

Things don't always work out for us in life, but if we let God into our hearts and into our lives, he will make things right for us in heaven. And if we are given gifts in this lifetime, let's use them unselfishly to help other people who aren't as well off as we are.

The Grateful Leper

In the time of Jesus, some people suffered from horrible skin conditions. They were known as lepers, and they weren't welcome in the towns and villages, not only because they looked horrible and were rather smelly, but also because people thought that the disease might be catching. So lepers usually lived outside of the villages and stayed out of everyone's way as much as possible.

But one time when Jesus was going into a village, he was met by a sad sight—ten men, all suffering from leprosy. They stayed well back, but they cried out in loud voices, "Jesus, please take pity on us!"

Jesus felt sorry for them. He told them to go straight to the priests, and as they went, a miracle happened—they saw that their sores had completely disappeared. Their skin was smooth once again!

The excited men shouted and danced and leaped about in joy, and they made their way to the priests as quickly as they could.

But one of the men, as soon as he realized that he was healed, rushed straight back to Jesus, praising God at the top of his voice. He threw himself to the ground before Jesus and thanked him with all his heart.

Jesus looked down at the grateful man. "Didn't I clean ten men? Where are the other nine? Are you the only one to come back to thank God?"

Then he said kindly, "Go on your way now. Your faith has made you well."

It is easy to get carried away with excitement when something really good happens, but let us always remember to thank God for all the wonderful things he gives us and for his everlasting love.

The Humble and the Proud

One day, Jesus looked around at the crowd around him. There were many different kinds of people there—some were farmers or fishermen, others were craftsmen or market traders, but others among them thought themselves rather more educated, rather more important. Indeed, some among them thought very well of themselves, and so Jesus told a story about two men who went into a temple to pray. One of these men was a Pharisee, and the other was a tax collector.

Now, the Pharisees had very strong opinions about religion (in fact, they cared more about their religion than God!). They liked to think that they kept all of God's rules—every last one of them—and they felt that this made them rather special. They usually thought that they knew best! As for tax collectors, well, most people hated them because they got rich by taking money from other people and by giving it to the Romans (and people didn't like the Romans much either), and lots of tax collectors cheated and stole as well.

In the temple, the Pharisee stood by himself and prayed: "God, I thank you that I'm not like other people—robbers, criminals, adulterers—or even like this tax collector. I fast twice a week and give a tenth of all I get!" To be honest, it wasn't so much a prayer as bragging. The Pharisee thought he was very good and holy and far better than everyone else!

But the tax collector stood humbly at a distance. He would not even look up to heaven, but beat his breast and said, "God, have mercy on me, for I'm nothing but a miserable sinner."

Jesus looked around at those who were listening. "It wasn't the self-important Pharisee who earned God's love and forgiveness that day; it was the humble tax collector. For all those who show off and think themselves important will be humbled, and those who humble themselves will become important."

It doesn't matter how many good things we have done. We can never be as good as Jesus, so we really don't have anything to brag about. God wants us to be humble and to think about his goodness and not about ourselves.

Bags of Gold

Jesus told his followers a story about a man who was heading off on a long journey. Before he went, this man called his three servants to him because he wanted to leave all his money with them while he went so that they could make use of it, and he gave each of them a certain number of bags depending on their abilities. He gave one of them five bags of gold, another two bags, and one bag to the third.

Some time later he returned and called the servants before him to see what they had been up to. Imagine how delighted he was when the first servant said to him,

"Sir, I put your money to work, and with the five bags of gold you gave me I have made five more." The man was very pleased and told him that since he had been able to trust him with a few things, he would gladly put him in charge of many things.

Then the second servant told him that he had gained two more bags on top of the ones that had been given to him, and again, the master was pleased that he could be trusted and put him in charge of many things.

Last of all, the third servant spoke up. "Master," he said, "I know that you are a hard man, and I was scared, so I hid the gold in a hole in the ground so it would be safe. Here it is now," and he handed over the bag of gold.

The master was angry. "You have been wicked and lazy," he exclaimed. "You could at least have put my money in the bank so it could earn some interest!" He gave the bag of gold to the one who had ten bags and then had the worthless servant thrown out of the house!

God expects us to use whatever gifts he has given to us. If we do, he will give us even more, but if we don't, he may take them away and give them to someone who *will* use them!

The Last Will Be First

Jesus told a parable: "The kingdom of heaven is like the vineyard owner who had lots of work that needed to be done in his vineyard, so he went out early one morning to the marketplace to see if he could hire some workers. There were plenty of men hanging around there hoping for work, so the vineyard owner offered them a certain amount of money for the day and set them to work.

"Later on that same day, he went back to the marketplace, hired more men, and told them he'd pay them whatever was right. He did the same thing at lunchtime and in the afternoon. When he went back to the marketplace at about five o'clock in the afternoon, there were still some men hanging around there, and he asked them what they were doing wasting their time lounging about. 'No one offered us any work,' the men said (which was a bit of a silly thing to say, since the owner had already been to the marketplace several times that day looking for people to hire!). The owner told them that they could come and work for him in his vineyard.

"The vineyard bustled with activity, and lots of work was done that day. When evening came, the owner called his foreman to him and told him to pay the workers, beginning with the last ones hired.

"The workers who were hired late received the same amount that had been promised to the first workers. So when those at the back of the line, the ones who had been hired first, came to receive their pay, they expected to get more because they had worked longer, but they were given exactly the same amount as the others.

"At this, they began to grumble. 'They only worked for one hour,' complained one, 'but you've given them the same as those of us who worked all day long in the blazing heat! How is that fair?'

"The owner answered, 'I'm not being unfair. Didn't you agree to work for this amount? I paid you what we agreed. I want to give the one hired last the same as you. Don't I have the right to do what I want with my own money? Or are you annoyed because I'm being generous?'

"So the last will be first, and the first will be last."

Some people will serve God all their life, and their reward will be everlasting life in heaven. Then there are those who do bad things and don't listen to God—until the very end of their life, when they feel truly sorry for the things they have done and let God into their heart. God will reward them with everlasting life in heaven too! Everyone who believes in God and opens their heart to him will receive the same reward—not because God is being unfair to those who have believed in him all along, but because he is being generous to all of us!

The Wicked Tenants

Jesus knew that the priests and the Pharisees and the leaders were trying to catch him in an error all the time. They would hang around when he was talking, but they weren't really listening to what he had to say. They had hardened their hearts to his message and would not believe that he was the Son of God.

Jesus knew that the priests and the Pharisees often obeyed the letter of the law but didn't understand the real meaning of the law—they said the right things without really letting God into their hearts and without accepting Jesus.

He told them a story. "There was once a man who had two sons. He went to the older one and said, 'Son, go and work in the vineyard today.'

"'I don't want to,' grumbled the son, but later he changed his mind and went.

"The father went to his other son and asked him the same thing.

"'Yes, sir,' answered the son, but he didn't actually go."

Jesus looked around, "Which son actually did what his father wanted?"

"The older one," they answered.

You see, what we *do* is more important than what we *say* we will do!

Jesus told another story…

"There was once a man who planted some grapes, rented the vineyard to some farmers, and then went away. At harvest time he sent a servant to collect his share of the fruit. But instead of giving him what they owed him, the wicked tenants beat the servant and sent him away with nothing!

"The man found it hard to believe what had happened, so he sent another servant, but again they beat him and sent him away empty-handed. He sent a third, and that one was killed!

"In the end, the owner decided to send his own beloved son. 'Surely they will respect him,' he said to himself.

"But when the tenants saw him coming, they plotted among themselves. 'This is the owner's son,' they said. 'If we get rid of him, we will become the new owners!' And they threw him out of the vineyard and killed him."

Jesus looked at the priests and Pharisees who were listening. "What do you think the owner of the vineyard will do to the tenants when he finds out?"

"He will kill them and give the vineyard to others who will treat him fairly and give him his share," they replied. But when they realized that Jesus had really been talking about them, they felt tricked and angry!

You see, God sent many special people, such as Moses and David and Isaiah, to tell people how much he loved them and to warn them to mend their ways. But the people didn't want to listen, and so, at last, he sent his own Son, Jesus…

God has given us so many chances. Let's not miss this one.

Jesus and the Children

Jesus loved little children, for they are good and innocent. He was always surrounded by children, and sometimes his disciples tried to shoo them away. They thought he had far more important things to do than be bothered by pesky little kids!

But Jesus had other ideas. "Don't ever stop little children from coming to me," he told them sternly. "The kingdom of heaven belongs to them and all those who are like them."

The disciples still didn't understand. They began arguing about which of them was Jesus' most important helper.

"I do the most!" said one.

"No, I do!" said another.

"Well, I look after the money, so where would you all be without me?" claimed a third.

Jesus looked at them in despair and sighed. They were missing the point. God didn't care about who was the cleverest or the most powerful or the best at cooking or the best at anything at all, in fact. We don't need to do anything special to earn God's love except allow him into our lives and into our hearts. And the disciples shouldn't have been thinking about themselves so much anyway.

Jesus told them, "If you want to be first, you must be last, and you must be the servant of all." If we want to be great in God's sight, we need to put others first and ourselves last—we should try to be a servant rather than expect other people to look after us!

Jesus beckoned one of the little children to come to him and put his arm around him.

"You see," he said, turning to the disciples, "whoever welcomes this child in my name welcomes me, and whoever welcomes me welcomes the one who sent me. For it is the one who is least among you who is the greatest. To enter heaven, you must be like a little child!"

Zacchaeus up a Tree

Zacchaeus lived in Jericho, and there are two things that you should know about him—he was rich, and he was rather on the short side. Zacchaeus was rich because he was a tax collector, and nobody liked tax collectors, but they especially didn't like the rich ones because it was obvious how they had become rich—by cheating and stealing some of the precious taxes and lining their own pockets. So Zacchaeus wasn't very popular in Jericho.

Now, on this particular day, the streets of Jericho were lined with people eager to catch a glimpse of Jesus. They had all heard about this amazing man who could make people well again and perform all sorts of other miracles and tell wonderful stories, so everyone who could spare the time had crowded onto the streets to see if they could catch a glimpse of him or hear him speak.

But you need to remember the second thing about Zacchaeus—he was short! And that was a particular problem today. No matter where he went, he couldn't see over the heads of the people in front—every last one was taller than him. Even some of the children were taller! And when he tried to squeeze his way through, they all glared at him. Nobody wanted to make room for a cheating tax collector!

Zacchaeus hopped about in frustration. He could hear the buzz of the crowd getting louder, so he knew that Jesus was nearby. He was going to miss everything!

Then he had a great idea. At the side of the road stood a tall, sturdy sycamore tree. No sooner had he had the thought than he shimmied up the tree trunk and perched himself precariously on an overhanging branch. He did feel rather wobbly up there—and he got some very strange looks, especially from the birds—but he didn't care! He could see everything that was happening from up there.

Zacchaeus watched excitedly as Jesus walked slowly down the street. He was going to pass right under the tree! Then he realized that Jesus wasn't going to pass right under the tree after all—no, he was going to stop there!

Zacchaeus almost fell off the branch when Jesus stopped right below and said, "Zacchaeus, come down now. I must stay at your house today."

Zacchaeus couldn't believe his ears. Jesus knew his name! And he wanted to stay at his house! He scrambled down as fast as he could and bowed low before Jesus. All around him the crowd muttered angrily—Jesus was going to visit a sinner yet again!

Zacchaeus could hear their grumbling, but he was already a changed man. He said to Jesus, "Lord! I'm going to give half of everything I have to the poor, and if I have cheated anybody out of anything, I'll pay back four times the amount!"

Then Jesus turned to the crowd and said, "It is lost people like Zacchaeus that I came to save. Today he has found salvation!"

Jesus knows your name too, and he will never give up on you!

Martha and Mary

There were two sisters who lived in a little house in a village called Bethany. Their names were Martha and Mary. One day, Jesus and his disciples were passing through the village, and they stopped to visit!

Martha and Mary were thrilled. But they went about things rather differently. Martha rushed to sweep the floor and tidy the chairs and lay the table and prepare the food… and Mary just sat on the floor by Jesus' feet, not wanting to miss a single word he said.

At last, Martha could stand it no longer! "Lord," she said to Jesus, "won't you tell Mary to help me? There is so much to get ready, and she is sitting there doing nothing while I do all the work!"

"Martha, Martha," said Jesus in a soothing voice, "you are worrying about all these small things, but do you know they're not really what is important? Your sister understands what is truly important, and it won't be taken away from her."

Of course Jesus wasn't saying that we should laze around doing nothing and leaving the work to others. But there are times when we need to stop rushing around and look instead at the big picture. If Jesus came to your house to stay, would you spend your time preparing a wonderful feast with lots of fancy dishes—or would you rather spend your time with Jesus himself, listening to him and loving him?

Always remember that Jesus is the most important thing in our lives—and don't get so busy with other things that you forget to spend time with Jesus.

Lazarus Lives!

One sad day, Jesus received a message from Martha and Mary, telling him that their brother, Lazarus, was dreadfully ill. Jesus was very fond of the sisters and their brother, but he did not leave where he was for two whole days.

"Why are you still here?" asked the disciples, for they expected him to rush back to the village.

Jesus told them, "This has happened in order to bring glory to God and to the Son of God."

By the time Jesus arrived at the sisters' village some days later, Lazarus was dead.

Martha came to meet Jesus on the road, weeping bitterly. She had loved her brother so much! "Oh, Lord," she cried, "if you had been here, my brother would not have died. But I know that even now God will give you whatever you ask."

Then Jesus said gently, "He will rise again. Everyone who believes in me will live again, even though he has died. Everyone who lives and believes in me will never really die. Martha, do you believe this?"

And Martha answered quietly, "Yes, Lord. I do believe that you are the Son of God."

Martha went back home and told Mary that Jesus was here, and Mary went to meet him, and her relatives went with her. When Jesus saw Mary weeping and all the other relatives, he wept too. He felt so sorry for their grief.

He asked to be taken to the cave where Lazarus had been laid, and he told the men to open it.

Now, Lazarus had been dead for four long days, but the men did as Jesus had asked them without question. When the cave was open, Jesus stood at the entrance and prayed and gave thanks to God. Then he said loudly, "Lazarus, come out!"

Everyone watched in silent wonder as a figure slowly emerged from the dark cave, his hands and feet wrapped with strips of linen and a cloth around his face. It was Lazarus, and he was alive! His sisters rushed to help him. The tears rolling down their cheeks were now tears of joy—their beloved brother had been given back to them!

For Jesus, nothing is impossible!

The Expensive Perfume

It was some time later, on an evening shortly before Passover. Jesus was having dinner with his disciples and friends in Bethany. Mary came up to him, carrying a large jar of expensive perfume. Kneeling before him, she carefully poured the perfume on his feet, using her own hair to wipe them. The whole house was filled with the wonderful fragrance.

But not everyone was pleased. One of the disciples, Judas Iscariot, was angry. "What a waste!" he complained. "That perfume was worth a year's wages. We could have sold it and given the money to the

158

poor!" (That all sounded very well meaning, but the truth was that Judas Iscariot didn't really care that much about the poor. In fact, he was a thief. His job was to look after the money for Jesus and the disciples, and he used to help himself whenever he felt like it!)

Jesus hushed him. "Judas," he said gently, "what Mary did was lovely. You will always have the poor, and you can help them any time you want. But you won't always have me. People will remember Mary's kindness to me."

For Jesus would not be with them in this way for much longer. The final stage of his time on earth was about to begin.

Jesus Enters Jerusalem

It was a springtime Sunday in Jerusalem, and the city was packed to bursting. It was a special time, for it was the week of the Passover festival, and everyone had gathered to celebrate.

There was something else to celebrate too, for Jesus had come to Jerusalem. People had heard about the miracles he had performed, and while the religious leaders weren't too keen on him, many of the people saw Jesus as their true king, and they tried to give him a king's welcome.

He probably didn't look much like a king though. Where was the chariot? The trumpets? The servants? No, when Jesus entered Jerusalem he was riding a young colt, a humble donkey that his followers had fetched from a nearby village.

But that didn't stop the excitement. Some of the crowd threw their cloaks or large palm leaves on the dusty ground before him. Others waved the palm leaves high in the air, and they cried out, "Hosanna to the Son of David! Blessed is the king who comes in the name of the Lord—the King of Israel!"

Many of these people hoped that Jesus would be their king—a leader who would free them from the Romans. They didn't understand that his kingdom wasn't in this world but in heaven—Jesus came to earth to die for our sins so that we could join him in his heavenly kingdom—and soon their elation would turn to bitterness and disappointment when he did not do what they wanted him to do.

But for now, they were excited and were making quite a stir. Some of the religious leaders didn't like it, and they told Jesus to stop his followers from making so much noise. Jesus looked at them. "If they remain silent," he said, "then the stones themselves would cry out!"

Jesus knew his mission on earth was almost finished. And he knew that in a short time these people cheering would turn against him.

Before coming to Jerusalem, he had told his friends that when he came to the city, all the things that the prophets had spoken about would come true. The Son of Man would be condemned to death. He would be mocked and hurt and crucified, but three days later he would be raised to life. Right now, the disciples didn't understand the truth. But Jesus knew exactly what was going to happen to him, and he never, ever thought about not going through with it. For he knew it was God's will and that it was the only way to save those he loved for all time.

Troublemaker

As far as the priests and Pharisees and the Jewish elders were concerned, Jesus was causing trouble in Jerusalem. The very first thing he did when he came into the city was to visit the temple and throw out all the greedy, cheating money lenders and market traders

who had set up shop there to make money out of the poor people who came to make sacrifices to God. Jesus' fans might think that the temple was a far nicer place now, perfect for prayer and teaching, but as far as the priests were concerned, Jesus had no right to do what he had done (and they had made their fair share of money out of those money lenders and market traders too!). They particularly hated the fact that people were flocking to the new, improved temple to listen to Jesus and to come to him for healing, rather than to them.

No, Jesus was a rebel and a troublemaker and a pain in the neck, and he had to go! And if they didn't get onto it themselves, and he stirred up a real rebellion, then they were worried that Rome would turn its beady eye on Jerusalem, and who knew what would happen then! Especially at Passover, for after all, Passover celebrated the time when God brought the Israelites out of slavery in Egypt into the Holy Land, so it was a bit of a touchy issue with the Romans.

For the priests and Pharisees and elders, the only problem with getting rid of Jesus (apart from the small fact that technically he hadn't done anything illegal!) was that the people in the city loved him so much, and they didn't want to make them angry, especially during the festival. So they went about trying to catch him in an error, sending spies to follow him and trap him into saying something that they could arrest him for then and there. But Jesus saw through all their tricks and refused to play their game.

In the end, they decided to just arrest him anyway, but that wasn't so easy, for he always seemed to be surrounded by his followers. They needed some help—and that help came from one of Jesus' own disciples!

Judas Iscariot was dishonest. He looked after the money for Jesus and the rest of the disciples, and he kept some back for himself instead of giving it to those who needed it. In the end, his greed made him do a very bad thing. Judas went to the chief priests in secret and asked them how much they would give him if he delivered Jesus into their hands.

The priests couldn't believe their ears! They knew that Judas was one of Jesus' closest, most trusted friends. They offered him thirty silver coins, the going price for a common slave…and Judas accepted! As soon as he had left the temple, the priests rubbed their hands in glee. They couldn't believe it had been so easy! Now they had someone else to do their dirty work for them.

From then on, Judas was simply waiting for the opportunity to hand Jesus over.

Two Small Coins

Jesus was sitting in the temple, watching people put money in the collection boxes as offerings to God. Many rich people put in lots of clinking coins, making sure everybody knew how good they were being! Then along came a poor widow, her young children in threadbare clothes and bare feet. She put in two small copper coins. Together, they were worth less than a penny!

Jesus turned to his disciples. "Did you see that poor widow?" he asked. "The truth is, she gave far more than anyone else here today." The disciples looked puzzled. Surely her coins had been almost worthless!

Jesus tried to make them understand: "All those rich people had so much money that it was easy for them to give huge offerings—they still had plenty left. But that poor widow gave everything she had to give. She clearly loves God with all her heart and trusts him to look after her, for she gave him everything she had."

Like a Servant

It was nearly time for the Passover feast, and a kind man had set aside a room in his own house for the disciples to prepare for it. That night, when they were eating, Jesus left the table, wrapped a towel around his waist, filled a basin with water and then, kneeling on the floor, began to wash and dry the disciples' feet like a servant.

The disciples were speechless. In those days people's feet got ever so dirty because they wore open sandals on dusty roads, but it would usually be the job of the very lowest servant to go about kneeling on the floor and washing the dirt away. What on earth was Jesus doing?

So when Jesus knelt before Simon Peter, the disciple threw up his hands in horror, "Lord, you mustn't wash my smelly feet! That's not your job!"

Jesus replied gently, "You don't understand what I'm doing, Peter, but soon you will. Unless you let me wash away the dirt, you won't really belong to me."

When Jesus said this, Peter begged him to wash his hands and head too! But Jesus answered, "If you have bathed, you only need to wash your feet; your body is clean."

Then Jesus washed the rest of the disciples' feet, one by one, until they were all clean.

When he finished, he said to them, "Do you understand what I was doing? You call me 'Lord' and 'Teacher,' and that is what I am— but I'm your servant too. The master isn't more important than the servant. I washed your feet, so you should wash one another's feet too."

Jesus had washed their feet like a servant so that they could learn to do the same for one another.

Jesus was sad and troubled. He knew he would soon have to leave his friends. "Soon, one of you will betray me," he said sorrowfully. The disciples looked at one another in shock. Who could he possibly mean? They all loved him and would follow him to the ends of the earth!

Well, that was true for eleven of them. But one was about to betray Jesus—and do you know, Jesus felt sorry for him! The others had no idea what Jesus was talking about. They had no idea who the traitor was, but Jesus said softly to Judas Iscariot, "Go and do what you have to do," and Judas left. But the others still didn't understand—they probably thought he was going off to do something with the money (which I suppose he was).

Now Jesus handed around some bread, saying, "This is my body, which will be broken." Next, he passed around a cup of wine, saying, "Drink this. It is my blood, which will take away sin." He wanted them to remember this time with him, and he hoped they would one day understand what he was really telling them.

Then he said that he would soon be leaving them.

At this, the disciples called out in dismay. Simon Peter cried out, "But Lord, where are you going? Why can't I follow you? I would lay down my life for you a hundred times over!"

"Would you, my friend?" asked Jesus gently. "And yet you will disown me three times before the cock crows!" Peter was horrified. He knew—he just knew—that he would never do such a dreadful thing.

173

Jesus knew how upset the disciples were at the news he had given them. He tried to comfort them.

"My dear friends," he said, "I am going ahead to prepare a place for you in my Father's house. You will know how to find your own way there."

"How?" cried the disciples in confusion.

"I am the way and the truth and the life," replied Jesus. "The only way to the Father is through believing in me. If you really know me, you will know my Father as well.

"And just as my Father has loved me, so have I loved you. And I give you this command: Love one another, just as I have loved each of you, and everyone will know that you are my disciples. There is no greater love than to lay down one's life for one's friends.

"And don't lose hope if everyone seems out to get you, if the whole world seems to hate you—just remember that it hated me first. It is because you don't belong to it that it will hate you!"

Jesus wanted his disciples to never ever give up, however much the world seemed against them. And he wants you to never give up too. If people are ever mean to you because you love Jesus—well, you are in the best company of all!

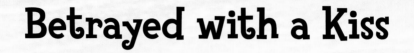

Betrayed with a Kiss

That night, Jesus and the disciples left the hustle and bustle of the busy city and went to a quiet garden filled with olive trees set on a hillside. Jesus wanted to pray to his Father. He asked Peter, James, and John to keep him company and to wait nearby while he went off on his own to talk to his Father.

His heart was filled with sadness, for he knew what was about to happen, and he was dreading it. In misery, he cried out, "Oh, Father, is there any other way? Does it have to happen like this?" Yet his very next words were, "But let it be not as I want, but as you want."

What was going to happen would be terrible beyond belief, but Jesus knew that God wasn't making him do anything—he had chosen freely to do it. He trusted in God and knew that this was the only way to save God's children. He needed to take all their sins upon himself, and he needed to take their punishment too. He would be their scapegoat so that they could be free from their sins and free to be close to God again. It was the plan, and Jesus believed in the plan. But he knew it was going to be so, so hard.

Sadly he returned to Peter, James, and John. He felt even more alone when he found his friends fast asleep. They couldn't even stay awake with him for one hour!

He spoke to his Father two more times that night, and each time the disciples couldn't keep their eyes open and dozed off. The last time, when he came back to them he awoke them to say, "The hour has come. You need to get up, for the one who betrayed me is here!"

177

And so he was, for at that moment a huge crowd of people burst into the quiet garden with lanterns and swords and heavy clubs. And at the head of them all was Judas Iscariot, come to earn his precious silver coins. He had told the chief priests that he would kiss Jesus so that they would know whom to arrest, and as Judas approached him, Jesus said sadly, "Oh, Judas, would you betray the Son of Man with a kiss?"

When he realized what was happening, Simon Peter was filled with anger, and he struck out with his sword, cutting off the ear of one of the crowd that had come to do the high priest's dirty work.

"No, Peter," said Jesus, making him put away his sword and healing the man's ear. "Don't you think my Father would send a host of angels to save me if I asked him to? This has to happen—how else can everything the prophets said about me be fulfilled?"

Then he turned to the soldiers. "I'm the one you have come to find," he said quietly. "Let these others go. You had no need to come here with swords and clubs. You could easily have taken me when I was in the temple courts."

The disciples were filled with despair. They could see clearly now that Jesus wasn't going to try to escape or fight, and as he let himself be arrested, they ran away in fear and went into hiding.

By the flickering light of their torches the guards led Jesus through the streets of Jerusalem to the house of Caiaphas, the chief priest of the Jews. He was the one who had sent them to arrest Jesus, and he was waiting for them there, along with the other high priests who made up the council. All this was very wrong. The Jewish law of the time didn't allow trials to take place at night, and definitely not in someone's house. But that didn't bother the priests—they had already decided Jesus was guilty!

Now, they needed to find a reason to order Jesus' execution, but they had a small problem—they didn't have any evidence against him. Not to worry, they thought. It was easy enough to persuade some people to come and tell lies about him. Unfortunately for them,

though, the "witnesses" that they found couldn't seem to agree on the same story, so they were back to square one.

Caiaphas decided that the easiest thing would be to get Jesus to commit blasphemy (blasphemy is speaking about God in a disrespectful way).

"So," he said to Jesus, "tell us, are you the Son of God?"

"You have said it yourself," Jesus answered. "And I will tell you this: You will see the Son of God sitting at the right hand of the Almighty God, riding on the clouds of heaven."

"Enough!" the high priest cried. "This man claims to be the Son of God. This is blasphemy—this man must die!"

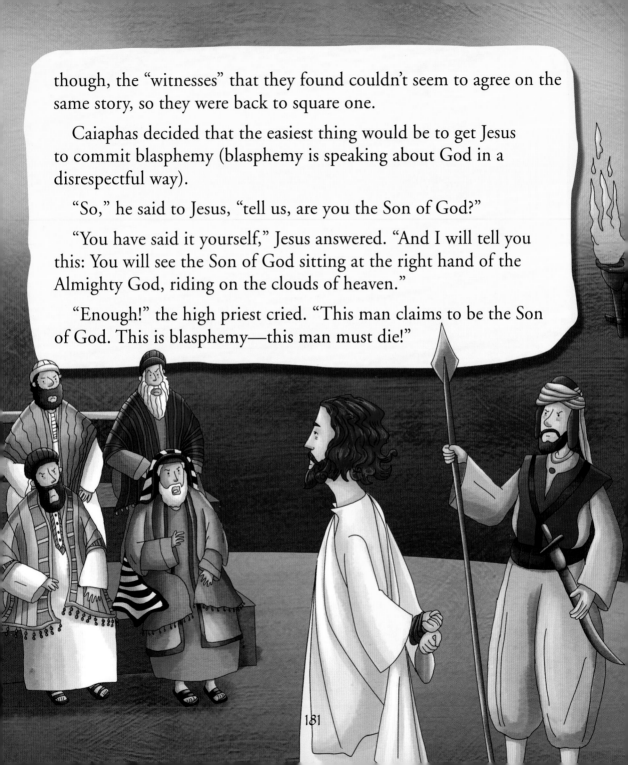

A Cock Crows

While all this was happening, Simon Peter was waiting miserably outside in the courtyard. When the soldiers had taken Jesus to be questioned, Simon Peter had followed them to the house of the high priest, and now he waited with a heavy heart and filled with fear, along with the guards warming themselves at the fire. As one of the servant girls was walking by, she caught sight of Peter by the fire. It was pretty dark in the courtyard, but there was enough torchlight to see by, and the man looked a bit familiar. She peered more closely at Peter's face. Then it dawned on her: "Weren't you with Jesus of Nazareth?" she asked. "I'm sure I saw you with him."

"No, no! You've got the wrong man!" Peter hissed quietly, hoping no one else had heard, for he was terrified about what might happen if they thought he was one of Jesus' disciples.

The girl simply shrugged and walked away, but a little while later she crossed the courtyard on her way back. She glanced at Peter again, then she said to one of the guards, "Don't you think he looks like one of Jesus' followers?"

"I told you, I don't have anything to do with him!" babbled Peter in a panic before the guard could reply.

But now everyone was looking at him. "You must be one of them," said one of the guards. "I can tell from your accent you're from Galilee."

"I swear I've never even met him!" cried Peter, his heart racing.

At that very moment, a cock crowed, and Peter remembered what Jesus had said only a few hours ago, and he broke down and wept in dismay. How could he have betrayed Jesus like that! He felt as if his heart had broken in two.

Pilate Washes His Hands

"This man must die!" Caiaphas had said, but it wasn't as straightforward as that.

Unfortunately for the high priest, the Jews weren't allowed to execute anyone—the Romans liked to keep that sort of thing all to themselves. And more than that, the Romans wouldn't really care much about whether or not Jesus thought he was the Son of God, because they didn't believe in God anyway.

So the priests had to come up with another plan. They decided to tell the Romans that Jesus was calling himself "King of the Jews." The Romans would certainly care about that! The Jews weren't allowed to have any kings—they were all subjects of the mighty Roman emperor! If Jesus claimed to be a king, then that was treason—and in Rome, instant death was the penalty for treason!

So Jesus was taken before Pontius Pilate, the Roman governor. Now, to be honest, Pilate was out for an easy life. He asked Jesus a few questions, read a few reports, and could see perfectly well that Jesus wasn't a threat at all. Jesus about to lead a rebellion of Jews against Rome? Not a chance! The man was clearly innocent, but that wasn't what the crowd wanted to hear.

You see, by now, quite a crowd had gathered. The rumor had spread: Jesus of Nazareth was on trial for his life. Those very same people who, just a few days before, had cheered and waved as Jesus entered Jerusalem, had now been fed lies (and maybe bribes) by the priests and Pharisees and wanted blood! In fact, it was quite a mob.

Pilate saw just one way out. It was Passover, and at Passover it was the custom to release one prisoner. The crowd had a choice of two prisoners to vote for (not that they could really vote!): Jesus of Nazareth (the one who had healed lots of people and told wonderful stories about love and forgiveness and mercy) or Barabbas (currently in prison for rebellion and murder).

Hmm…

Should have been a fairly obvious choice, don't you think?

But no, the crowd had been whipped into a frenzy by the priests and Pharisees and the leaders, and they all started chanting, "Free Barabbas! Free Barabbas!"

"But what has Jesus done wrong?" asked Pilate.

In reply, the crowd shouted, "Crucify him! Crucify him!"

Pilate was dismayed, but he didn't want to start a riot. He didn't care enough about justice to actually do anything about it. Instead, he called for a servant to bring him a bowl of water, and he washed his hands in it. "It's your call," he was saying to the people. "I didn't have anything to do with it!"

As I said, Pilate definitely wanted an easy life. He cared more about himself than anything else.

A Shadow Falls

Soldiers led Jesus away. "So you're king of the Jews, then?" they said mockingly. "Well then, let's make sure you look the part!" They dressed him in a purple robe, the color worn by kings, and put a crown of sharp thorny branches upon his head. Then they beat him and spat in his face before putting him back in his own clothes and leading him through the streets toward Golgotha, the place where he was to be crucified.

They made him carry the wooden cross on his back, but it was large and heavy, and Jesus had been dreadfully beaten and he hadn't rested all night. When he could carry the cross no longer, they snatched someone from out of the crowd to carry it for him. And so the dreadful procession made its way out of the city to the hill of Golgotha.

There on the hillside, soldiers nailed Jesus to the cross and placed above his head a sign saying, "JESUS OF NAZARETH, KING OF THE JEWS." As they raised the cross, Jesus cried, "Father, forgive them. They don't know what they're doing."

Two criminals were crucified beside him.

"If you're so special, why don't you save yourself? And save me too while you're at it!" one sneered.

But the other told him to be quiet. "Look," he said to him, "we're here because we deserve to be. But Jesus hasn't done anything wrong." Then he turned to Jesus and said, "Please remember me when you come into your kingdom," and Jesus promised he would be with him that very day in Paradise.

As Jesus hung there on the cross, down below the guards drew lots to see who would win his clothes (after all, he didn't need them anymore), and the priests and Pharisees taunted him—"If you come down from the cross now, we'll believe in you!" they mocked.

Of course Jesus could have chosen for all this to stop anytime he wanted. But he stayed there because he chose to—because he loved these people so much and wanted to save them from themselves.

At midday, a shadow passed across the sun, and dark clouds filled the sky. For three long hours darkness covered the land as though it were the middle of the night. At three o'clock in the afternoon, Jesus cried out in a loud voice, "My God, why have you forsaken me?" He had always been so close to his Father, they were one, but now he bore the sins of all the people in the world, and so he felt all alone for the first and last time.

Then he let out a great cry—"It is finished!"—and with these words, he gave up his spirit and let himself die.

At that moment the earth shook, and in the city the curtain in the holy temple was torn from top to bottom, for Jesus, through his death, had removed the barriers between God and man. There is nothing now that comes between us and God.

Back on the hill, when the Roman soldiers felt the ground move beneath their feet and saw how Jesus passed away, they were deeply shaken. "Surely he was the Son of God!" whispered one in amazement.

Though Jesus had always meant for this to happen, his friends were heartbroken at his death. They took his broken body down from the cross and carefully wrapped it. Then they took him to a tomb carved out of rock and laid his body inside.

But the priests and Pharisees remembered that Jesus had spoken about rising again, and so they asked Pilate to put guards on the tomb, and they had it sealed with a massive stone so that nobody could get in or out. They wanted to make sure that none of his followers could pull some sort of clever stunt with his body to try to fool people!

"That's the end of Jesus!" said the chief priests smugly.

But, of course, they were wrong…

The Empty Tomb

Three days later, early in the morning, before the sun had fully risen, Mary Magdalene and some other women went to anoint the body of their beloved teacher. As they walked sadly along the dusty path, they wondered among themselves whom they could persuade to open the tomb for them, for the stone was far too big and heavy for them to move it themselves.

But just as they came near to the tomb, the earth shook beneath their feet, the guards were thrown to the ground, and the women saw that the stone had been rolled away from the entrance. And inside the tomb, shining brighter than the sun, was an angel!

The terrified women fell to their knees, hands over their eyes, for the angel was too bright to look at (and they were too scared anyway!). But the angel said to them, "Why are you looking here for someone who is alive? This is a place for dead people! Jesus isn't here—he has risen! Don't you remember that he told you this would happen? Have a quick look, and then run and tell his disciples that he will meet them in Galilee just as he promised."

So the women hurried away in excitement to tell the disciples the news, afraid yet filled with joy.

Later on that same day, Mary Magdalene stood weeping quietly outside the tomb. Peter and one of the other disciples had come, had seen the strips of linen, and had gone away again, not knowing what to think, whether to be happy or sad. Now Mary was here by herself. The angel's words had filled her with hope, yet she felt so alone. All she wanted was to see Jesus one more time.

Just then she heard the sound of footsteps behind her. A man asked gently, "Why are you crying? Who are you looking for?"

This must be the gardener, she thought. Surely he would know where the body was. And she begged forlornly, "Sir, if you have moved him, please tell me where he is, and I'll get him."

The man only spoke her name, "Mary," but instantly she spun around. She recognized that clear, gentle voice!

"Teacher!" she gasped. Surely this was a dream! Was he really, truly there? And she reached out toward Jesus with her arms wide open.

Jesus said, "Dear Mary, you mustn't hold on to me, for I have not yet gone to my Father. Quick! Go and tell the others!" So Mary rushed off with the amazing news that she had seen Jesus alive! The disciples were never going to believe her!

Alive!

That same evening the disciples, all except Thomas, were huddled around a table in a dark room talking about the incredible events of the day. They had closed the shutters and locked the door because they were scared that the Jewish leaders would try to arrest them, but their thoughts were all on Jesus. Could he really be alive? They shook their heads in disbelief. Maybe the women had imagined it all.

Suddenly Jesus was with them in the room! The men started in shock. Some of them glanced at the door—no, it was still locked! He hadn't come in that way! So what was this, a ghost? And some of them were scared.

"Friends, friends," said Jesus soothingly, "why do you look so worried? Don't you believe your own eyes? It really is me."

Some of the men still looked uncertain. "Look," said Jesus, "look at my hands and feet. Here are the scars from the nails. See for yourselves!" Then he asked, "Is there any food around here?" and as the disciples watched him eat, he looked at them and laughed. "Do you still think I'm a ghost? Would a ghost be eating dinner here with you?"

And then all the disciples laughed too, and they crowded round Jesus, hugging and kissing him with tears of joy running down their faces. They felt as if their hearts would burst with happiness.

But Thomas, as we said, wasn't there. Can you imagine how he felt when his friends told him what had happened? He just couldn't believe it. He just couldn't. "Unless I see the holes with my own eyes, and put my finger where the nails were, I won't believe," he said angrily. Because, of course, he did want to believe.

Just one week later, the disciples were all together again, Thomas too, when suddenly Jesus was among them again. The first thing he did was turn to Thomas. "Well, Thomas, do you believe now?" he asked. "Come nearer, look for yourself, touch the wounds with your own hands. Stop doubting, Thomas—and believe!"

Thomas fell to his knees, overcome with joy. "Oh, Lord, I do believe!" he cried out, bursting with happiness.

Jesus smiled at him. "Thomas, you believed only because you saw me yourself with your very own eyes. Think about the people who believe without even seeing. How blessed will they be!"

Lord, help us to believe, even if we can't see you with our own eyes!

The Ascension

Jesus and his friends were on a hillside outside Jerusalem. It was time for him to leave the world. The disciples were sad that Jesus was leaving, but in the days and weeks since his resurrection, he had made many things clearer to them and had told them a little about what the future would hold. They knew that he wasn't really leaving them—he was just going ahead to prepare the way for them. And he had promised he wouldn't be leaving them alone—he was going to send them help.

Jesus had told his disciples what to do. "You must stay here in Jerusalem for now," he had said, "and wait for the gift that my Father has promised you, for soon you will be baptized with the Holy Spirit. Then you must spread my message not only in Jerusalem and the places near here, but in every country throughout the world!"

So now, as they stood upon the hillside, the disciples were filled with hope and strength and belief. Jesus held up his hands to bless them and then, before their eyes, he was taken up to heaven, and a cloud hid him from sight.

As his friends stood looking upward in wonder, suddenly two men dressed in white stood beside them. "Why are you looking at the sky?" they asked. "Jesus has been taken from you into heaven, but he will come back again in the same way that he left!"

Jesus has gone to heaven to prepare a place for us, and one day he will come again to take us to our new home so that we can live forever in God's love.

Flames of Fire

It was ten days since Jesus had been taken up to heaven. The disciples* were gathered together in a room early one morning waiting for something to happen. Mind you, they didn't know what that "something" was! All they knew was that they had lots of work to do spreading the message that Jesus had brought and the amazing news about what his death and resurrection really meant—but that Jesus himself had told them to wait here in Jerusalem until God sent them a special gift. So here they were, waiting patiently, all twelve of them (for they had chosen a man named Matthias to join them to take the place of Judas Iscariot).

Suddenly the house was filled with the sound of a mighty rushing wind coming from heaven. The men looked around in wonder, filled with excitement, and then gasped as flames of fire seemed to rest on each person there. It was the Holy Spirit sent by God to guide and help them in their special mission, making a home inside their hearts. They couldn't see the Holy Spirit—just like the wind—but they could feel it deep within them.

* The disciples became known as apostles, or messengers, for they were chosen by Jesus to pass on his message of good news.

The men were all filled with the Holy Spirit, and they began to speak in different languages—languages they had never spoken before or studied! Can you imagine that? All of a sudden being able to speak Greek or Mandarin or Basque or Urdu? Wouldn't that be amazing? Wouldn't it be a miracle?

Hearing the commotion, a huge crowd gathered outside. You can imagine how taken aback they were when the apostles came out of the house and began to talk to them in different languages!

"What's going on?" they exclaimed in amazement. "How are they doing this?"

There were people there from Asia and Egypt, from Libya and Crete, from Rome and Arabia—and each and every one of them was being told all about God in their very own language. And yet all the apostles were from Galilee!

Of course, there are always some people who can't take things seriously. Some people only wanted to make fun of what was happening.

"They've all had too much wine!" they mocked. "They're drunk!"

209

Peter stepped forward confidently. "Listen!" he said clearly so that everyone could hear him. "Don't be ridiculous! It's nine o'clock in the morning—of course we're not drunk! We have been filled with the Holy Spirit! Just a few weeks ago Jesus from Nazareth died on a cross. Yet ask any one of us, and we can tell you that God has raised Jesus to life! We have all seen him with our very own eyes!

"You see, this was all part of God's plan. You know deep down that Jesus really was sent to you by God—think about all the miracles he performed, all the signs he showed you. Jesus was handed over to you, and you rejected him and had him killed by evil men. But God planned it all. Jesus died, but death could not hold him! God made Jesus your Lord and Messiah!"

The people looked worried and unhappy. What had they done? And how could they ever make it better?

As Peter looked at their faces, he knew what they were feeling. "If you really are sorry," he went on, "then repent. Be baptized in the name of Jesus Christ, and the bad things that you have done will all be forgiven. And just like us, you will receive the wonderful gift of the Holy Spirit! This promise is not just for you, but for your children, too, and for people who are far away—God's gift is for everyone!"

Many, many people believed in Jesus that day. Soon the word spread, and more and more people learned the wonderful news and joined God's own family.

211

Getting Into Trouble . . . and Out Again!

Of course, not everybody was happy with the way things were going. The Jewish priests and leaders thought they had gotten rid of Jesus, but now they must have been feeling as though they had stirred up a hornet's nest! Instead of one troublemaker, now they seemed to have many—and it was getting worse all the time! Maybe if his annoying followers had just stuck with talking, things would have been alright, but oh, no, not them…

One day, Peter and John were making their way to the temple to pray when they spotted a man begging outside the gates. Now, this poor man had been lame ever since he was born, and that made it very difficult to get a job, so he spent every day outside the temple, hoping that some kind passerby would be able to spare him a coin or two. When Peter and John stopped in front of him, he looked up hopefully.

213

"I'm afraid I don't have any money," said Peter, and the man's heart sank. Yet Peter hadn't finished speaking. "But," the apostle went on, "I can give you something far better!" As the lame man looked puzzled, Peter continued, "In the name of Jesus Christ, I order you to get up and walk!" And to everyone's astonishment—especially the beggar himself—Peter held out his hand and helped him to his feet. He couldn't believe what was happening—he was actually standing up on his own two feet! Flabbergasted, the man tried a few cautious steps, and then a few more, and a few more still. Then he jumped up and down a bit and gave a little leap in the air.

"Oh, Lord!" he cried in delight and gratitude, "how truly wonderful you are!"

Then he carried right on walking straight into the temple to thank God over and over again for the amazing thing Peter had done!

The people could hardly believe that this was the same man who had sat outside the temple every day to beg. They all crowded round Peter and John.

"Hold on a minute," said Peter. "We didn't make this man walk all by ourselves. God did it. It was faith in the name of Jesus that healed this man! So praise God!"

The people were amazed. They listened to what Peter had to say, and then they all rushed off to tell their friends and neighbors.

Naturally, it wasn't long at all before the Jewish leaders heard about the miraculous healing and heard the apostles talking to the people. They were so angry that they threw them into prison, saying, "Who gave you the right to do this?" which was a bit silly really, and probably sounded sillier still when Peter calmly replied that it was by the name of Jesus Christ that the man had been healed. Anyway, the next day they had to let them go—after all, everyone had seen the lame man walk, so what could they do, apart from tell them to keep their mouths shut?

But things went from bad to worse as far as the Jewish priests and leaders were concerned. Nobody seemed to want to listen to them anymore. All that anybody could talk about were the apostles and their wonderful words and healing. So they threw the apostles back in prison again (they really weren't very clever, were they?)—but do you know what happened this time? In the middle of the night they had a very special visitor—an angel! The angel opened the prison doors and led the men out and told them to go back to the temple and carry on spreading the good news.

Well, when the priests called for the apostles to be brought before them the next day, they got a very nasty surprise.

"They just disappeared!" said the terrified guards. "Honestly—the doors are still locked!"

When the apostles were finally found (at the temple, obviously), the priests accused them of disobeying their instructions. But Peter and the others bravely replied, "We must obey God rather than human beings!"

218

Some priests wanted to have them executed, but one said wisely,
"If they are just stirring up rebellion, in the end it will all fizzle out.
But if they really are from God, then you won't be able to stop them,
and will find yourselves fighting against God!"

So the apostles were released under strict instructions not to talk
about Jesus anymore—but of course they did! And more and more
people listened to them, and more and more people believed.

Saul Sees the Light

The new Christians had many enemies, but one of the people most out to get them was Saul of Tarsus (sometimes he went by the name of Paul, which was the Roman version of his name).

Now Saul was a Pharisee, and like the other Pharisees, he loved rules. He thought that being a Jew was all about following rules, and he thought he did a better job of it than almost anyone else. He hated the followers of Jesus because they were saying that the rules weren't important anymore, that the only important thing was believing in Jesus. No way!

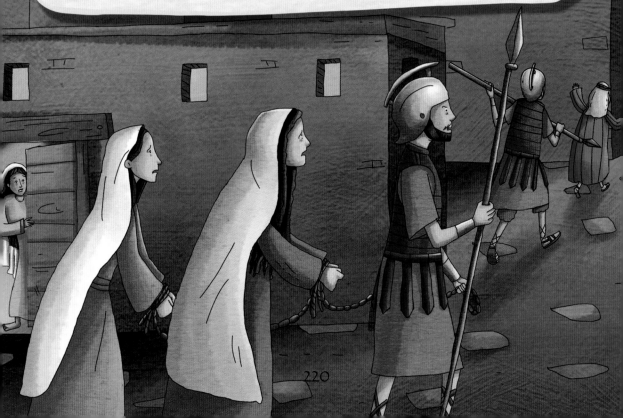

And so Saul did everything he could to stop the Christians from spreading their message and causing trouble. He would go from house to house, pounding on the doors in the dead of night, dragging men and women out of their houses and throwing them into prison. It was his duty to get rid of all the vermin in this wonderful holy city! But he also knew that lots of Christians were leaving Jerusalem to escape him, and wherever they went they were spreading their poison. So he decided to head off to Damascus where many of them had gone. They weren't going to get away from him that easily!

Saul was making his way along the dusty road to Damascus, probably thinking about all the troublesome people he was going to catch, when suddenly, a blinding light from heaven flashed down. Saul fell to the ground, covering his eyes. What was happening?

Then he heard a voice say, "Saul, why do you keep on persecuting me?"

Saul began trembling. He thought he knew who was speaking, but he had to ask.

"I am Jesus," replied the voice, just as he had known it would. "Get up and go into the city, and someone will meet you and tell you what to do."

Saul had some guards with them, and they didn't have a clue what was happening! They had heard the voice, but they didn't see any light—what was going on, and why was Saul down on the ground with his eyes tight shut?

Saul struggled shakily to his feet, but when he opened his eyes, he couldn't see a thing! His guards had to take him by the hand and lead him into the city. There he stayed for three days without eating or drinking, spending his time in prayer. He had so much to think about—everything he had believed had been wrong. He had thought that what he was doing was pleasing God—now he had found out that he had been hurting him. But there was still time to change his ways and try to undo the dreadful things he had done.

You see, God had great plans for Saul. Saul was going to be the one to spread the news far and wide—farther than anyone else—and so God sent a Christian named Ananias to the house where he was staying. When he got there, Ananias laid his hands on Saul, and it was as if scales had fallen from his eyes, and Saul could see once more! And now, filled with the Holy Spirit, he saw everything so much more clearly.

Saul (or Paul) began to spread the good news about Jesus in Damascus, and people could hardly believe their ears.

"Didn't this man used to be our enemy?" they would ask in astonishment. "Is it really the same man?" But while his old enemies became his friends, his old friends soon became his enemies. In the end, it wasn't safe for him to stay in Damascus any longer, but he couldn't just walk out the front gate—the soldiers were looking for him. Do you know how he escaped? His friends hid him in a large basket and carefully lowered it over the city walls under cover of night! Once he was safely down, Saul jumped out of the basket and made his way back to Jerusalem. Now that he had met Jesus and had seen the light, he realized that all the rules he had been so hung up on before were not important. The only important thing in life was knowing Jesus.

With this truth in his heart, Saul went on to become one of the greatest of all the apostles.

The Sheet of Animals

Do you ever have strange dreams? Have you ever wondered if they were trying to tell you something? Well, one day Peter had a dream, and it was very strange indeed.

Peter was lying on a rooftop by the sea. He had been praying to God, but it was hot on the roof, and he had dozed off. In his dream, he could a huge white sheet being lowered from heaven by its corners. The sheet was filled with all sorts of mammals, reptiles, and birds. Looking closely, he realized that they weren't just any old animals. They were all creatures that Jews were forbidden to eat, for they were considered "unclean." It was one of the many things that made them different from Gentiles—people who weren't Jews. Peter was a Jew, and he had always followed the rules. He knew what he was allowed to eat and what he wasn't.

So imagine his surprise and shock when he heard God's voice saying, "Get up, Peter. Kill and eat."

"Surely not, Lord!" Peter replied in horror. "I have never eaten anything unclean in all my life!"

The voice said, "Don't call impure what God has made clean."

This happened three times, and then the sheet was pulled back up to heaven.

Peter knew that God wasn't telling him to go out and eat lizards or butterflies or vultures. What was he telling him?

It was at that moment that Peter awoke to the sound of knocking. He was about to understand what the dream had meant.

Downstairs were three men sent by an officer named Cornelius. Although Cornelius was Roman, he and his family all believed in God. He was a good man and tried to live a good life. He tried to help the poor, and he spent time praying to God—and God had answered! God had told him to have Peter brought to his house.

As soon as Peter saw that the three men at the door were Gentiles, he invited them in, for now he understood his vision. The very next day he did as they asked and went with them to Cornelius's house in Caesarea, where Cornelius's friends and family had gathered.

Peter looked around. These people were Gentiles, but they were all ready to listen to what he had to say about Jesus. They were no different from the Jews, no less worthy—no less "clean"! For it is sin which makes a person unclean, and when Jesus died on the cross, he cleansed everything! God wanted his message to be passed on to the Gentiles just as much as to the Jews. He wanted to give his love to them too.

"God doesn't show favoritism," Peter told his eager listeners. "He doesn't care if you are a Jew or a Gentile. He will welcome anyone who believes in him and tries to follow his laws."

While he was talking about Jesus, the Holy Spirit came. God had given the Gentiles the same gift that he had given to Jesus' special disciples. God's message is for all the people of the world, not just for Jews. That is what Peter's vision had meant!

God doesn't look at the outside of people—he doesn't care about the color of their skin or what country they come from. He looks at what is in our heart, and his love is for every single person in the world.

Spreading the Good News

The apostles dedicated their lives to spreading the good news—that trusting God's grace to save us through his Son, Jesus, our sins are forgiven and we are promised an everlasting home in heaven.

Although Paul (Saul usually went by his Roman name these days) was not one of the original twelve apostles, he traveled far and wide as a missionary, traveling to different people in different lands, to pass on the wonderful message about Christ. He spoke to everyone, not just the Jews, just as God had commanded. Sometimes he traveled on his own, but other times he traveled with friends. Sometimes they were welcomed, and sometimes they were not! Either way, he had many strange adventures on his journeys.

Once, some people in a place called Lystra (in modern-day Turkey) decided that when Paul and his friend Barnabas healed a lame man, they must be gods! They wanted to offer them sacrifices and put wreaths around their necks! Barnabas and Paul had a hard job explaining that they were ordinary men and trying to tell them about God!

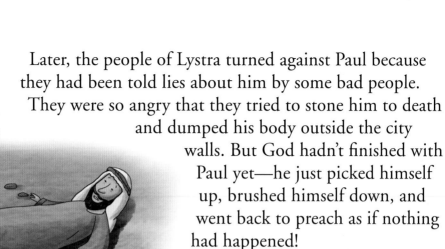

Later, the people of Lystra turned against Paul because they had been told lies about him by some bad people. They were so angry that they tried to stone him to death and dumped his body outside the city walls. But God hadn't finished with Paul yet—he just picked himself up, brushed himself down, and went back to preach as if nothing had happened!

Then there was the time that Paul and his friend Silas healed a slave girl in Philippi who had been ranting and raving like a mad thing because she had been possessed by an evil spirit. You would have thought that the slave girl's owners would have been happy that the poor girl was back to normal, but instead they were furious. You see, when she had been possessed by the spirit, she had been able to foretell the future, and her owners had made a whole pile of money out of her predictions! Now she had nothing to say, and the money had dried up!

They had Paul and Silas dragged before the city magistrates. The crowd joined in the attack, and Paul and Silas were whipped and beaten and thrown into prison, with their feet locked in stocks.

It was midnight. Paul and Silas were lying in the stocks. The chains were tight and the wood was heavy, but they didn't despair. Instead, they were praying and singing hymns. The other prisoners could hardly believe their ears. The usual sounds in prison were of groaning and weeping—not singing!

Suddenly a violent earthquake shook the prison, the cell doors flew open, and everyone's chains came loose! The jailor was more terrified than anyone. He knew that his prisoners would escape and he would get into big trouble, but Paul told him that they wouldn't run away. When the jailor had calmed down enough to listen to him, he invited Paul and Silas back to his own house because he wanted to learn about Jesus, and he wanted his family to learn about him too. They became Christians that very night!

234

Lots of other strange and wonderful things happened to Paul, but as time went on, he knew it was time for him to return to Jerusalem. He wanted to help the Christians there.

His friends thought he was crazy. "You can't go back to Jerusalem," they protested. "As soon as you enter the city you'll be thrown into prison—or worse! Please don't go!" they pleaded as he got ready to board a ship heading back to Jerusalem.

But Paul shook his head sadly. "Please don't try to change my mind. This is what I have to do. I'm ready not only to be put in chains for Jesus, but to die for him."

Even though he knew in his heart that hardship and suffering were ahead of him, Paul would go wherever God wanted him to go. Paul's friends wept as he sailed away. They knew that they would never see him again.

Paul traveled to Jerusalem, and sure enough, just as his friends had feared, he was arrested and thrown into jail. The trouble was, no one really knew what to do with him. He hadn't actually broken any laws! But time passed and still he was in prison. In the end he demanded to be seen by Emperor Caesar himself in Rome—all Roman citizens had that right. And so he found himself on board a ship yet again.

Shipwrecked!

Paul was traveling to Rome aboard a ship. To start with, the voyage wasn't unpleasant—Julius, the Roman centurion in charge, was kind to Paul, and some of Paul's friends were on board with him. But bad weather and stops delayed their voyage, and the stormy season was upon them all too soon and forced them to take shelter in a harbor. It really wasn't the right time of year to be sailing, and Paul tried to warn the captain that if they carried on, they would be heading for trouble. But the captain ignored his advice, and the ship set sail.

Soon they found themselves in the middle of a dreadful storm. For days the ship was at the mercy of the angry sea, dragged along by the towering waves and fierce winds. The terrified crew began throwing first the cargo and then anything that they didn't absolutely need over the side to try to save the ship, but it didn't help, and after several days passed without sight of the sun or stars, all hope seemed lost. What else could they do?

Everyone was sitting around glumly, feeling sorry for themselves and certain that they were going to end up at the bottom of the murky ocean. But then Paul spoke up. "I wish you had listened to me when I warned you that this would happen, but even so, there's no point in giving up hope like this. You need to be brave. Everything is going to work out—God has promised that we will all reach land alive. Only the ship will be lost. So cheer up and put your faith in God as I do. It's going to be alright—I promise!"

After two whole weeks at the mercy of the storm, the sailors sensed that they were approaching land, but they were scared that they would be dashed upon the jagged rocks. Some of the sailors tried to leave in one of the lifeboats, but Paul told the captain and Julius that everyone had to stay with the ship to be saved, so they cut the ropes that held the lifeboat and let it drift away.

Paul also made sure that everyone had something to eat. For two whole weeks they had all been too terrified to think about food, but he knew that they had to keep their strength up.

As the sun began to peek over the horizon, a beach finally came into sight. Everyone was so excited! But just as things seemed to be looking up at last, suddenly the ship struck a sandbar. The bow stuck fast, and the ship began to be broken to pieces by the surf!

The soldiers were worried that some of the prisoners might swim away and escape, so they were planning to kill them, but Julius stopped them. He ordered everyone who could swim to make for land, and he told those who could not swim to cling to pieces of the broken ship and float ashore.

There were two hundred seventy-six people on board that ship, and every last one of them reached the shore safely—just as God had promised!

Even when things seem impossible, even when we feel like giving up hope, God can always help us to weather any storm.

Letters of Love

In the end, Paul did finally reach Rome, and while he waited for his case to be heard by the emperor, he was allowed to live by himself, with a soldier to guard him. He wasn't allowed out, but he could have visitors, and so he was able to carry on spreading the message.

Paul was also a wonderful letter writer. People don't write so many letters nowadays. We pick up the phone and call someone or maybe drop them an email or even a quick text. But Paul couldn't do any of those things! And he couldn't get to see all his friends. So instead, Paul wrote letters—wonderful letters of advice and encouragement and love.

Often the friends he was writing to were brand-new Christians whom he had met during his travels. Paul tried to encourage and help them in their important work—they were trying to set up new churches in their towns and cities, and sometimes they had problems. Paul told them that if times seemed hard, they should not give up.

"Whatever hardships and suffering you are feeling now will be more than made up for in heaven!" he wrote. "And remember, often it is our suffering that helps us to get stronger in our faith, so keep your eyes on heaven and rejoice in the Lord!"

He told them to remember that it is faith in Jesus that will save us—"Don't get hung up on obeying lots of little laws," he said. "That isn't the way to get close to God. We can never obey enough laws to be truly good, so we can't be saved by being good, but we can be saved by believing in Jesus. Don't be slaves to the law—Jesus has set us all free, so stay free!"

Paul's words are as useful and important today as they were when he wrote them.

Corinth was a busy seaport, and all kinds of people lived there, doing all sorts of different things. Paul didn't want the people in the new church there to argue among themselves about who was the most important or who served God best.

"You're all important!" Paul wrote. "Maybe you can speak in lots of different languages so that you can tell lots of people about God's message. But that doesn't make you more important than someone who can heal people who are sick. And how about the person who has a real gift for teaching? You all need to work together—as a team.

"Or think about it like this—you are all like different parts of one body. Are the arms more important than the mouth? Or the head than the feet? Have you ever tried to stand on your head all day? I wouldn't recommend it! Even those parts of the body that don't seem to have such a big role, or seem weaker, are just as important."

Paul was saying that we should all respect and take care of one another and work together without quarrelling. God has given us all different gifts, different skills and talents. So let's not get big-headed when there's something that we can do well—especially when everything we have is a gift from God in the first place! It doesn't make us better than anyone else. No, instead let's concentrate on using God's gifts to do his work and to help those around us. Each and every one of us is a precious part of the body of Christ—let's all work together!

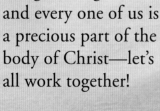

244

For Paul, nothing was more important than love—love for God, love for Jesus, and love for one another. Paul told the Corinthians, "If I could speak every single language in the world, even if I could talk with angels, but I didn't love others, I would be no more than a noisy gong or a clanging cymbal. If I had the gift of prophecy, or knowledge, or such great faith that I could move mountains, it would mean nothing if I didn't have love. I could give every last thing that I owned to the poor and suffer great hardship, but it would all mean nothing if I didn't feel love for the people I was doing it for.

"Love is patient and kind. It isn't jealous, boastful, proud, or rude. It doesn't insist on having its own way, or become cross, or want revenge, or feel happy when someone else fails. Love protects, and trusts, and hopes. It is steady and true, and it never, ever gives up. Three things will last forever—faith, hope, and love—and the greatest of these is love."

Love gives meaning to everything!

Put On God's Armor!

Ephesus was a bustling port city in the Roman province of Asia Minor, which today is Turkey. It was an important trade city, and Paul had set up the church there. It had been a wicked city with many bad people in it before Paul had come to tell them about Jesus, but through God's kindness it had been saved.

Paul sent its people some wonderful words of encouragement: "Be strong in the Lord. Our real enemies aren't made of flesh and blood—your real battle is against the devil's clever tricks, and to fight that battle you need to put on every piece of God's armor to be prepared.

"Then you can stand your ground confidently, with the belt of truth round your waist and the breastplate of righteousness on your chest. Let your feet be fitted with the readiness that comes from the gospel of peace, and take up the shield of faith. Put on the helmet of salvation and take hold of the sword of the Spirit—the word of God."

What a wonderful image! If we hold on to the truth that the Bible tells us, then we are well prepared to face Satan, the "father of lies." If we always choose to do what God says is right, then Satan can't harm us. If we feel ready and at peace because we are assured of God's love for us, then we can stand firm and ready, whatever is coming at us. If we have faith in God, then our faith will protect us from seeds of doubt. Jesus came to earth to save us, and accepting this is our ultimate source of protection. All these things help defend us. Paul suggests only one weapon of attack—but it is the Bible, and that is more than enough, for it is the Word of God!

God's Word and God's love are our protection against all that life can throw at us—they truly are our armor. So let's put on all of God's armor, every last piece, and prepare to do battle!

250

God Is Love

Other writers also had inspiring words to say about faith.

The apostle James wrote, "What good is it to say you have faith if you don't show it by what you do? Words aren't enough, and faith isn't enough—not unless good things come of it."

Peter went on to say, "You face hardship and suffering—but don't despair! Instead, be glad, for these trials make you partners with Christ in his suffering. They will test your faith as fire tests and purifies gold. And remember that there is wonderful joy ahead! Don't be disheartened if it seems a long time in coming—God is being patient, for he wants everyone to repent. But the day of the Lord will come unexpectedly, so be prepared!"

The apostle John wrote, "God is love. He loves us so much that we are called children of God! He showed how much he loved us by sending his one and only Son into the world so that we might have eternal life through him. Since he loved us that much, let us make sure that we love one another so that God can live in us and we can live in God. And as we live in God, our love will grow more perfect, and when the day of judgment comes we will not have to fear anything.

"Perfect love drives out all fear! We love one another because he loved us first. All love comes from God!"

"I'm Coming Soon!"

The very last book of the Bible is Revelation. Many believe it was written by the disciple John. The author had an amazing vision to pass on: He had seen the Son of Man, with hair as white as snow, eyes like blazing fire, and a voice like rushing water. The Lord wanted John to send a message to the churches that had been set up across the land, to correct and encourage them.

But that wasn't all. John was also sent a vision of the future…

In his vision, John finds himself before the throne of God and the heavenly court. He sees a scroll with seven seals in the right hand of God, which could only be opened by the Lamb of God, by Jesus himself. And when those seals are opened, dreadful things happen to the world. John sees famine and plague, rivers of blood and terrible beasts—but however bad things get, God's beloved children are kept safe, and in the end, everything evil will be destroyed and God's kingdom will reign.

John wrote, "Then I saw a new heaven and earth, and I saw the Holy City coming down out of heaven like a beautiful bride. I heard a loud voice speaking from the throne: 'Now God's home is with his people! He will live with them. They shall be his people, and he will be their God. There will be no more death, no more grief, or crying, or pain. He will make all things new! For he is the first and the last, the beginning and the end.'

"And I was shown the Holy City, shining with the glory of God. It had a great high wall with twelve gates and twelve angels in charge of them. The city doesn't need a temple, because God and Christ will be there; it doesn't need the sun or the moon, because the glory of God shines on it, and the Lamb is its lamp. The gates will never be closed, because there will be no night there. And those whose names are written in the Lamb's Book of Life will enter.

"'Listen!' says Jesus. 'I'm coming soon!'

"Let it be so! Come, Lord Jesus, come soon!"

Nobody knows when Jesus is coming—but we know that he definitely is coming! Let's be ready for him, and let's say, just like John did, so many years ago,

"Come, Lord Jesus, come soon!"